Otho R Stubbs

The Red River Controversy

The Western Boundary Of The Louisiana Purchase

By C.A. Welborn

C. A. Welborn

ABOUT THE AUTHOR

Dr. Claude A. Welborn, retired professor of History from Southeastern Oklahoma State College, Durant, Oklahoma, has also been associated with the faculty at Paris Junior College of Paris, Texas, Delta State College of Cleveland, Mississippi; and served one summer term at Midwestern University at Wichita Falls, Texas.

A native of Electra, Texas, where he graduated from high school, Dr. Welborn received his Bachelor of Arts degree from East Texas State University. He taught schools at Mt. Vernon, Mesquite, Sealy, Driscoll, Woodville and Jourdanton, Texas. He received his M.A. degree from Oklahoma University and a Ph.D. degree from Texas University.

TABLE OF CONTENTS

CHAPTER I

The Louisiana Territory

The basin of the Mississippi River and much of the coastal region of the Gulf of Mexico, commonly known as Louisiana, were claimed by France on the basis of discovery and exploration by Robert Cavalier de la Salle on April 9, 1682.[1] In 1712 France made further claim to the region, by granting to Antoine de Crozat the exclusive right to trade there. This grant contains the first statement of limits of the vast region as they were understood by France. Louisiana was defined as comprising the drainage basin of the Mississippi River as far north as the mouth of the Illinois River but excluding Spanish claims in the Southwest.[2]

On November 3, 1762, France ceded this region to Spain, defining it only as the Province of Louisiana.[3] A few months later, on February 10, 1763, by the First Treaty of Paris signed between Great Britain, France, and Spain, the western boundary of the British possessions in the new world was placed in the center of the Mississippi River, thereby reducing Louisiana by the portion east of the Mississippi. Consequently, by these two treaties, France disposed of its possessions in North America, dividing them between Great Britain and Spain. The limits separating the possessions of these two countries were The Mississippi River, The Iberville River, and the lakes Maurepas and Pontchartrain.[4]

Great Britain then subdivided its share of the territory into Florida,

1 Emile Lauvriere, **Historie de la Louisane Purchase, 1763-1939**, p. 37; Binger Hermann, **The Louisiana Purchase and Our Title West of the Rocky Mountains**, p. 12.

2 Emile Lauvriere, **op. cit.**, p. 136.

3 Alcee Fortier, **History of Louisiana, 1512-1768**, Vol. II, p. 263.

4 William Cobbett, **Parliamentary History of England, 1753-1765**, Vol. XV, pp. 1291-1305.

the area south of the meridian which runs through the mouth of the Yazoo River and west of the Appalachicola River, and into East Florida, the region east of this meridian and south of the present north boundary of Florida.[5]

By the Second Treaty of Paris which closed the American Revolution in 1783, Great Britain reduced the area of West Florida by the cession of that portion north of 31 degrees north latitude to the United States; at the same time, East Florida and the remainder of Florida were ceded to Spain.[6] By the secret treaty of San Ildefonso in 1800, Spain returned Louisiana to France "With the same extent it now has in the hands of Spain and that it had when Spain possessed it, and such as it should be after the treaties subsequently entered into between Spain and other states."[7]

Immediately after the transfer was made known, President Thomas Jefferson inaugurated measures for securing free access to the sea through the Mississippi River by the purchase of New Orleans. James Monroe was appointed plenipotentiary to assist Robert Livingston who was our resident minister to France. By the time Monroe arrived in Paris, Napoleon had abandoned his plan to establish a French Empire in America; he proposed to sell all of Louisiana to the United States. The treaty of cession dated April 30, 1803, describes the territory simply as being the same as ceded by Spain to France by the treaty of San Ildefonso.[8] This lack of precise definition became the basis of a voluminous diplomatic correspondence between Spain and the United States over the western boundary of the Louisiana purchase.

On January 28, 1805, Monroe, envoy extraordinary, and Pinckney,

5 Adam Shortt and Arthur G. Doughty (eds.), **Documents Relating to the Constitutional History of Canada, 1759-1791**, Vol. I, pp. 105-109.

6 William M. Malloy, (ed.), **Treaties and Conventions, International Acts, Protocols, and Agreements Between the United States of America and Other Powers, 1776-1909**, Vol. I, pp. 583-595.

7 George Fred de Martens (ed.), **Recueil Des Principaux Traites d' Alliance de Paix, do Commerce, de Limites, de Exchange Conclus Par Les Puissance de L' Europe Tant Entre Elles, Du Avec Les Puissances et Etats Dans d' Autres Parties Do Monde Depuis 1701 Jsqu' a Present**, Vol. VII, pp. 337-339.

8 Malloy, **op. cit.**, pp. 337-339.

resident minister to Spain, reminded the Spanish Government of the necessity of settling a number of differences between the United States and Spain, one of which was the establishment of the boundary between the Louisiana Purchase and Spanish territory. The American principals proposed a joint commission consisting of five men; two to be appointed by Spain, two by the United States, and the fifth to be selected by the four. If the four representatives could not agree on the fifth, that member would be chosen by lot.[9]

The Spanish Foreign Minister, Juan Pedro Cevallos, refused to consider other questions but was willing to proceed with the survey of the boundary line. He suggested that the operation be divided into two divisions: one to mark the line on the east and the other to survey the boundary in the interior.

Monroe and Livingston replied that they would not consent to treat on part of the questions in dispute without the inclusion of the whole.[10] Cevallos again on February 16, 1805, reiterated the willingness of the Spanish Government to survey the boundary,[11] but the Americans, resorting perhaps to bluff, asked for a personal conference with the Spanish minister, intimating their disgust and threatening to terminate the correspondence.[12]

Cevallos, however, was not anxious to discontinue the correspondence, as was shown by a letter which he wrote to Monroe and Pinckney just six days later. He suggested the examination of the boundary of Louisiana which by nature was divided into two distinct parts: that on the Florida side and the other on the west between Louisiana and the interior province of New Mexico. He further proposed that these two lines should be considered separately.[13]

9 Monroe and Pinckney to Don Pedro Cavallos, Madrid, January 28, 1805, **American State Papers, Foreign Relations**, Vol. II, pp. 638-639.

10 Monroe and Pinckney to Cevallos, Aranjuez, February 5, 1805, **ibid.**, Vol. II, pp. 640-641.

11 Cevallos to Monroe and Pinckney, Aranjuez, February 16, 1805, **ibid.**, Vol. II, pp. 643-644.

12 Pinckney and Monroe to Cevallos, Aranjuez, February 18, 1805, **ibid.**, Vol. II, p. 644.

13 Cevallos to Monroe and Pinckney, Aranjuez, February 16, 1805, **American State Papers, Foreign Relations**, Vol. II, pp. 644-645.

Monroe and Pinckney countered with the offer that if Spain would cede its territory east of the Mississippi River to the United States and arbitrate the claims of the citizens and subjects of each power according to the convention of 1802, the United States would agree to the Colorado River as the boundary between Louisiana and Spain and would cede all rights to any territory west of that line. They further proposed a district or territory of thirty leagues on each side of the line, or, on the American side only if preferred by Spain, running from the Gulf of Mexico to northern Louisiana and remaining neutral and unsettled forever. As an additional inducement, they agreed to relinquish the claims of spoilation as a result of acts committed by the French within Spanish territory in the course of the war between France and England from 1793 to 1795 as well as all claims against the Spanish accruing from the suppression of deposits at New Orleans.[14]

Cevallos in his reply, denied Spanish responsibility for the American claims in regard to damages inflicted by the French upon American commerce, as well as that based upon the suspension of deposits at New Orleans. He stated that since the boundary line between the United States and Spain began at the Gulf of Mexico between the Caracut River and the Mermentao and ascended toward the north between the Adaois and Natchitoches rivers until it cut the Red River, the American proposal offered no advantage to Spain because Spain owned the land within the proposed bounds anyway.[15] Upon receipt of this communication, Monroe and Pinckney were convinced that no satisfactory settlement could be achieved at that time. Consequently, they terminated the correspondence on the question of boundaries.[16]

Discussions on the subject were suspended until 1815 when the Spanish ambassador, Louis Onis, reopened correspondence with Monroe who had become secretary of state.[17] In response, Monroe explicitly

14 Pinckney and Monroe to Cevallos, Aranjuez, May 12, 1805, **ibid.**, Vol. II, p. 665.

15 Cevallos to Monroe and Pinckney, Aranjuez, May 15, 1805, **ibid.**, Vol. II, pp. 666-667.

16 Monroe and Pinckney to Cevallos, Aranjuez, May 18, 1805, **ibid.**, Vol. II, p. 667.

17 Onis to Monroe, Washington, December 30, 1815, **ibid.**, Vol. IV, p. 422.

stated the claims of the United States to that part of Louisiana which was situated west of the Mississippi River as being the same as was held by France prior to the First Treaty of Paris, 1763. [18] He stated that the government of the United States, with respect to the western boundary of Louisiana, had never doubted since the treaty of 1803, that it extended to the Rio Grande. [19]

Onis replied by stating that the United States and Spain should proceed with good faith to mutually fix convenient limits between the two countries if this could be arranged. He contended that there would be no danger of violation by citizens of the two countries, and therefore no probability of controversies. Onis ridiculed the suggestion by Monroe that in return for all Spanish lands east of the Mississippi River, the United States would agree that Spain should have all lands between the Rio del Norte and the Colorado, as well as that area which lies between the Colorado River and Cape North, drawing a line by the Mermento River towards Natchitoches. Onis pointed out that this area was a part of the province of Texas and had been in uninterrupted possession of Spain without ever having been involved in any dispute between France and Spain. He rejected the offer on the ground that since the land to which the United States offered to relinquish title belonged to Spain, the United States was asking Spain to give its possessions east of the Mississippi River without compensation. Onis suggested that if Monroe should propose to make the Mississippi River the boundary line on an equitable basis, he would recommend it to his government. [20]

Monroe obviously either despaired of reaching an agreement with the Spanish Government and consequently felt that further discussion was useless, or he thought that by pursuing an independent course, Onis would compromise in order to reach some sort of settlement. Whatever his motive might have been, he forced the Spanish minister from a defensive position in the negotiations to one of leadership.

Onis assured John Quincy Adams, who had become Secretary of State in 1816, that his government would cede the two Florida's to the United States in consideration of an equivalent which might be useful to the

18 Monroe to Onis, Washington, December 19, 1816, **ibid.**, Vol. IV, p. 425.

19 Monroe to Onis, Washington, June 10, 1816, **ibid.**, Vol. IV, p. 430.

20 Onis to Monroe, Washington, January 16, 1817, **ibid.**, Vol. IV, p. 438.

Spanish Government. He reminded Adams that the exchange must consist of a territory which belonged to the United States, and which might offer invariable points marked by nature along the boundary line so that a future boundary controversy between the two countries would be impossible.[21]

In a letter written eleven days later, Onis stated that in spite of the fact that Spain had an original and undisputable right to all the lands situated on the west side of the Mississippi River, his government had resolved its claim to this area on the basis of possessions under the control of Spain when Spain acquired Louisiana in 1762 and possessions under the control of France at the time France made the cession to the United States. He further pledged that all treaties and conventions which had caused a change in the state of possession of the two nations before that date would be respected.[22]

Adams was adamant in his stand in regard to the matter. He again expressed the belief that it would be an unprofitable waste of time to enter once more discussions upon topics of controversy which had already been so thoroughly debated. As a basis for adjusting all differences between the two countries, he suggested that Spain cede all claims to territory east of the Mississippi River and establish the western boundary along the Colorado River from its mouth to its source and thence to the northern limits of Louisiana. If Spain was not inclined to establish the western boundary line at the time, he was agreeable to postponing that question to a future date.[23]

In response to this proposal, Onis, in a letter dated October 24, 1818, proposed that the limits of the respective possessions of both governments west of the Mississippi River should be designated by a line beginning at the Gulf of Mexico between the Mermento and Calcasievu rivers, following the Arroyo Hondo, between Adais and Natchitoches, crossing the Red River at 32 degrees north latitude and 39 degrees west longitude from London according to Melish's Map, and thence running directly north, crossing the Arkansas, the White and the Osage rivers

21 Onis to Adams, Washington, December 23, 1817, **ibid**, Vol. IV, p. 452.
22 Thomas Maitland Marshall, **A History of the Western Boundary of the Louisiana Purchase, 1819-1841**, Vol. II, pp. 70; Phillip Coolidge Brooks, "Diplomacy and the Borderlands," **California University Publications in History**, Vol. XXIV, pp. 1-218; Charles Wilson Hackett (ed.), **Picardo's Treaties on the Limits of Louisiana and Texas**, Vol. II, pp. 52-90 are all excellent treatments of the Treaty of 1819 and the boundary disputes.
23 Adams to Onis, Washington, January 16, 1818, **American State Papers, Foreign Relations**, Vol. IV, p. 464.

until it struck the Missouri River. From that point, the line would follow the middle of the Missouri River to its source so that the territory on the right bank of the river would belong to Spain and that on the left bank to the United States. The navigation on the Missouri, the Mississippi, and the Mermento rivers would remain free to both nations.[24]

On October 31, 1818, Adams replied that the boundary line west of the Mississippi River as was proposed by the Spanish minister could not be agreed to by the United States. He suggested that the line begin at the mouth of the Sabine River, follow the west bank of the river to the 32nd degree north latitude, the eastern bank and all the islands to belong to the United States; thence due north to the northernmost part of the 33rd degree north latitude to Red River; follow the course of Red River to its source, touching the chain of snow mountains in the vicinity of 37 degrees and 25 minutes west latitude and 106 degrees and 15 minutes longitude according to the Melish Map; thence along the summit of these mountains to the South Sea. He further suggested that the northern bank of Red River and all the islands belong to the United States.[25]

Onis accepted the mouth of the Sabine River as the initial point in the establishment of the line instead of the Mermento on condition that the line should run due north from the point of intersection with Red River to the Mississippi River and along the middle of that river to its source, leaving to Spain the territory lying to the right, and to the United States the territory to the left of this line.[26]

On November 30, 1818, Adams addressed a communication to Onis in which he conveyed the opinion of the President that he deemed it useless to pursue any further attempt at adjustment of the boundary line at that time. He therefore withdrew all commitments which had been made on the part of the United States Government in regard to the problem.[27]

By this firm stand, the negotiations on the subject of boundaries reached a crisis; Onis, consequently, waited for further instructions from

24 Onis to Adams, Washington, October 24, 1818, **ibid.**, Vol. IV, p. 529.

25 Adams to Onis, Washington, October 28, 1818, **ibid.**, Vol. IV, p. 530.

26 Onis to Adams, Washington, November 16, 1818, **ibid.**, Vol. IV, p. 532.

27 Adams to Onis, Washington, October 30, 1818, **ibid.**, Vol. IV, p. 545.

his government. With the arrival of these instructions on January 16, 1819, the Spanish minister immediately addressed a letter to Adams in which he stated that his government would agree that the boundary line should extend from the source of the Missouri westward to the Columbia River, and along the middle thereof to the Pacific Ocean.[28]

Adams replied to this proposal by a positive refusal to accept that part of the proposed boundary line from the source of the Missouri River to the Columbia River.[29] This refusal brought forth an alternate line which would start at the mouth of the Sabine River, as had been previously agreed, and run to the source of that river; thence by the 94th degree of longitude to the Red River; thence along the Red River to the 95th degree; thence due north to the Arkansas River and along the Arkansas to its source; thence by a line due west to the source of the San Clemente River in 41 degrees west latitude, and along that river to the Pacific Ocean.[30]

On February 6, 1819, Adams altered his previous proposal by setting the boundary line at the mouth of the Sabine River, following the course of that river to 32 degrees north latitude, the eastern bank and all the islands in the river to belong to the United States and the western bank to Spain; from 32 degrees, the line would run to the northernmost part of 33 degree north latitude, until it struck the Red River, and along the south bank of that river to the northernmost point of the bend between 101 degrees and 102 degrees. From that point, the proposed line would follow the shortest path to the southernmost point in the bend of the Arkansas River; from there, along the south bank to the source of that river; thence along 41 degrees latitude to the South Sea. He further provided that should 41 degrees be either north or south of the source of the Arkansas River, then the line would run north or south, as the case might be, from the source to 41 degree north latitude, and along that parallel to the South Sea. Adams specifically provided that the whole line should be based upon Melish's Map of the United States, published

28 Onis to Adams, Washington, January 16, 1819, **ibid.**, Vol. IV, pp. 615-616.

29 Adams to Onis, Washington, January 29, 1819, **ibis.**, Vol. IV, pp. 615-616.

30 Onis to Adams, Washington, February 1, 1819, **ibid.**, Vol. IV, pp. 615-616.

at Philadelphia and improved to the first of January, 1818.[31]

Prospects for an agreement by that time seemed more favorable than they had been at any time during the entire discussion of boundaries. In response to Adams' letter of February 6, 1819, the Spanish minister replied three days later; he submitted a plan whereby the boundary line would begin, according to the Melish Map, with the mouth of the Sabine River, follow the middle of the stream to 32 degrees north latitude; thence along that parallel to where it strikes the Red River; thence following the course of that stream westward to 100 degrees longitude; thence along 100 degrees longitude west to the Arkansas River; thence along the middle of the Arkansas River to 42 degrees north latitude; thence westward along that parallel to the source of the San Clements River; thence following the course of that river to 43 degrees north latitude and thence by a line due west to the Pacific Ocean. The proposal further provided the line would follow the middle of the Sabine, the Red, the Arkansas, and the San Clemente rivers. Onis specifically stated that all islands in those rivers which were situated eastward of this line would belong to the United States, but that all these streams would afford free navigation to both nations.[32]

In a letter dated on February 13, 1819, Adams agreed to the proposed line with the exception that he insisted on the 103rd degree west from London instead of the 100th degree as Onis suggested; and, from the source of the Arkansas River, he proposed that the line run directly west to the South Sea rather than westward along 42 degree latitude to the source of the San Clemente River and thence by a line due west to the Pacific Ocean as Onis had suggested. In addition, Adams insisted that the line should follow the western bank of the Sabine River, and the southern banks of the Red and Arkansas rivers, thereby giving the United States complete control of the beds of those streams.[33]

As Onis was indisposed at this crucial point, negotiations were continued on the part of Spain through Hyde de Neuville, the French minister at Washington.[34] On February 15, 1819, Adams reiterated

31 Adams to Onis, Washington, February 6, 1819, **ibid.**, Vol. IV, pp. 615-617.

32 Onis to Adams, Washington, February 9, 1819, **ibid.**, Vol. IV, p. 617.

33 Adams to Onis, Washington, February 13, 1819, **ibid.**, Vol. IV, p. 620.

34 **Ibid.**, Vol. IV, p. 621.

orally his demands in regard to the points of disagreement pertaining to the boundary. On the following day, Neuville presented Adams with a copy for the statements which Adams had made in conference for verification, with the assurance that the French minister would confer with Onis and report his views.[35]

The French minister reported to Adams that Onis had agreed to accept that portion of the proposed line along the 100th degree longitude from the Red River to the Arkansas and the 42nd degree north latitude from the source of the Arkansas River to the Pacific Ocean but that he insisted on establishing the boundary along the middle of the rivers and that the navigation would be free to both countries.[36]

Neuville stated that Onis refused to accede to all the American demands because it was a point of honor which he could not abandon without humiliation. Adams assured him that he could see no humiliation in it; that they were to agree upon a boundary, for which purpose that bank of a river was more simple and less liable to occasion future controversy than the middle of a river. Adams further contended that it would be extremely difficult to ascertain the middle of the rivers throughout their courses; that it would take a century to establish the line and divide the islands between the two nations. He predicted that citizens of the United States would more likely settle in the islands than would Spanish subjects, that by establishing the boundary such that the islands would be within the bounds of the United States at that time, would eliminate future controversies.[37]

Adams so convincingly argued this point that Neuville agreed that his view of the subject removed all ground for objection on the point of honor. The French minister promised Adams that he would attempt to convince Onis on the point provided that should the Spanish minister agree to place the boundary along the banks, Spanish settlers would have the right to navigate the rivers.[38]

On February 18, 1819, Onis called upon Adams with a draft of a treaty

35 Neuville to Adams, Washington, February 16, 1819, **ibid.**, Vol. IV, p. 622.

36 Charles Francis Adams (ed.), **Memoirs of John Quincy Adams,** Vol. IV, pp. 250-251.

37 **Ibid.,** pp. 250-251.

38 **Ibid.,** pp. 254-256.

which he had drawn after his having conferred with President Jefferson at which time he stated that the President had agreed to make certain changes, one of which placed the line in the middle of the rivers.[39] On the following day, a cabinet meeting was held to consider the changes which were desired by Onis. Since there were about 200 American families settled south of the Red River, the cabinet was of the opinion that the boundary should follow a chain of mountains running, according to the Melish Map, parallel to the Red River about 30 miles south of that river. The secretary of state conferred with the Spanish minister in regard to the matter, but Onis would not discuss the point. The cabinet then agreed to permit Spanish subjects to navigate the Sabine, Red, and Arkansas rivers but insisted on placing the boundary line along the south banks of the Arkansas and Red Rivers and the west banks of the Sabine River.[40]

After the cabinet meeting, Adams called Neuville to his office to report the decision of the cabinet in regard to boundaries and navigation; he insisted that the treaty must positively be signed before the following Monday since the President would deliver his message to the Congress on the Tuesday following. He suggested that if negotiations on the subject should not be concluded by that time, the President would so inform the Congress in order that it might take such measures as it might deem advisable before the close of the session of Congress.[41]

Onis called on Adams on February 20, 1819, to tell him that he must accept the treaty since the United States Government would have it so, though he still thought that Adams should accept the middle of the rivers as the boundary line rather than the west bank of the Sabine and the south banks of the Red and Arkansas rivers. Adams observed that there was not time left for further discussion; that the United States had yielded so much that Onis would certainly endear himself to his government by his having gained so much in this treaty. The Spanish minister assured the Secretary of State that he had been a most difficult person to deal with; in fact, more difficult than the President.[42]

The boundary line as it was finally agreed upon was as follows:

39 **Ibid.**, pp. 264.

40 **Ibid.**, Vol. IV, pp. 266-269.

41 **Ibid.**, Vol. IV, pp. 266-269.

42 **Ibid.**, Vol. IV, p. 270.

11

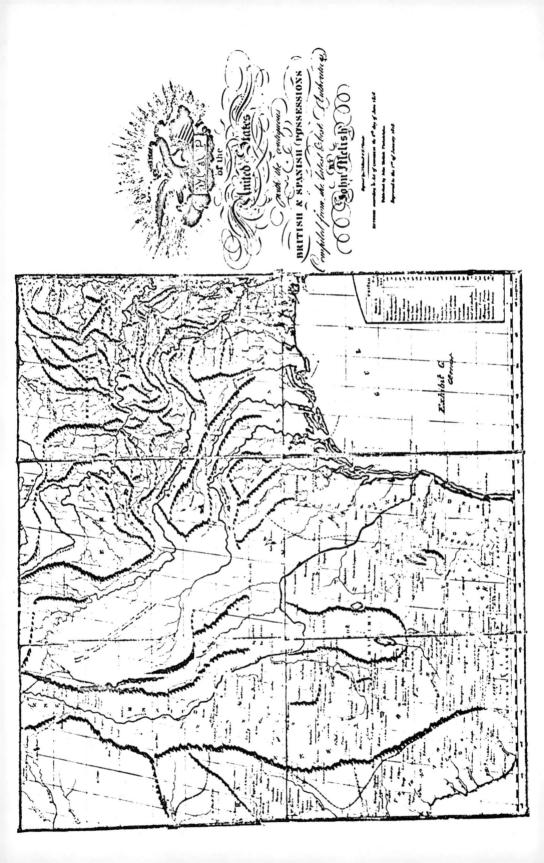

The boundary line between the two countries, west of the Mississippi, shall begin on the Gulf of Mexico, at the mouth of the River Sabine, in the Sea; continuing north along the western bank of that river, to the thirty-second degree of latitude; thence, by a line due north, to the degree of latitude where it strikes the Rio Roxo of Natchitches or Red River then following the course of the Rio Roxo westward, to the degree of longitude one hundred west from London, and twenty-three from Washington; then crossing the said Red River, and running thence, by a line due north, to the River Arkansas; thence, following the course of the southern bank of the Arkansas to its source, in latitude forty-two degrees north; and thence by that parallel of latitude to the South Sea; the whole being as laid down in Melish's Map of the United States, published at Philadelphia, improved to the first of January, 1818.

The treaty further provided that in order to fix the line with more precision and to place the landmarks which should designate the limits of both nations, each of the contracting nations should appoint a commissioner and a surveyor who should meet at Natchitoches before the termination of one year from the date of ratification of the treaty for that purpose.[43] For political reasons, Spain delayed the ratification of the treaty, and consequently, it did not go into effect until February 22, 1821.[44]

43 **American State Papers, Foreign Relations**, Vol. IV, pp. 623-625.

44 Monroe to House of Representatives, Washington, February 22, 1822, **ibid.**, Vol. V, p. 127.

CHAPTER II

Negotiations With Mexico and The Republic of Texas

As Mexico won its independence from Spain on August 24, 1821, and since the Spanish territory west of the Sabine and south of the Red and Arkansas rivers became Mexican territory, no further effort was made toward putting the provisions of the treaty into effect.[1]

Undoubtedly the Mexican Government wondered whether the United States would abide by the provisions of the treaty of 1819 between the United States and Spain which pertained to the establishment of the boundary between the two countries. In a note dated February 15, 1824, and addressed to Adams, the Mexican minister, Jose Torrens, declared that the President of Mexico wished to remove all matters which might affect the peace and harmony between the two countries; that he had been instructed to ask that the limits between the United States and Mexico be fixed according to the third article of the treaty of February 22, 1819, with Spain. He proposed further that commissioners be appointed to survey the boundary line according to the third article.[2]

On March 26, 1825, Secretary of State Henry Clay instructed the United States Minister to Mexico, Joel Poinsett, that, although the treaty of February 22, 1819, between the United States and Spain had not been carried into execution, the United States considered it obligatory upon both the United States and Mexico since Mexico was an integral part of the Spanish Empire when the treaty was concluded. He stated further that difficulties might at some future time arise between the two countries from this line against which it would be desirable to guard. He expressed the opinion that the line along the Sabine River approached the city of New Orleans nearer than he wished. According to the treaty of 1819, portions of both the Red and the Arkansas rivers

1 **American State Papers, Foreign Relations**, Vol. IV, pp. 841-842.

2 Torrens to Adams, Washington, February 15, 1824, **House Executive Documents, Twenty-fifth Congress, First Session** (Serial 311) Doc. No. 42, Vol. I, p. 6.

were on the Mexican side; that navigation on these rivers as well as the Sabine was open to both countries; when the area adjacent to those rivers should become thickly settled, collision and misunderstanding might arise from the arrangement.[3]

Clay suggested that by changing the line to a point further west, the capitol of Mexico would be located more nearly in the center of the United Mexican States. As a further inducement, he emphasized the fact that such a change would leave the Comanche Indians located in the United States territory. Clay indicated, however, that he was not prepared to insist upon the change of the line by instructing Poinsett that, if he found that the Mexican Government was not willing to alter the line, Poinsett was authorized to agree to the recognition and establishment of the line as described in the third article of the treaty of 1819, and to the demarcation of it as was stipulated in article four of that treaty. In this event, however, he requested that a clause be inserted providing that each nation be responsible for the acts of Indians who lived within its borders.[4]

In his first conference with the Mexican minister of foreign affairs, Poinsett assured Louis Alaman that the United States expected to adhere to the treaty of limits concluded with the King of Spain on February 22, 1819; he suggested that in order to demonstrate its independence, Mexico might want to make another treaty which would be even more acceptable to both countries. Alaman indicated a willingness to the suggestion by proposing that a joint commission be appointed to survey the country and report on the possibility of a new line. Poinsett objected to the proposal on the ground that such action would delay the negotiations until after the meeting of the next American Congress. The conference was concluded by the statement from Alaman that his government would be unwilling to fix the limits on the exceedingly meager information which it then possessed.[5]

On July 18, 1825, Alaman clarified his position on the question of boundaries by stating that the final conclusion of a treaty embracing the establishment of a boundary line could not be effected in haste; he contended that the marking of a boundary, by its nature, and the

3 Clay to Poinsett, Washington, March 26, 1825, **ibid.**, p. 3.

4 Clay to Poinsett, Washington, March 26, 1825, **ibid.**, p. 5.

5 Poinsett to Clay, Mexico City, July 18, 1825, **ibid.**, p. 19.

particular difficulties which in that case attended such a work, both from the lack of topographical information and the necessity of making extended trigonometrical observations over a vast area, would require much time regardless of how diligent the two governments might be in forwarding the work.

He suggested that the two governments name commissioners who, on examining together the country within a given latitude and from sea to sea, might present exact information upon which the limits might be established. Alaman reasoned that his plan threw no obstacle in the way of the final conclusion of the subject since the information would be necessary to the running of the line regardless of whether it was gathered after or before the agreement on general principle. [6]

Poinsett replied that he could see only one serious objection to the proposal; that was the delay which would be incurred by the plan. He pointed out, as he had done before, [7] that should the President of the United States accede to the plan, he could not appoint such commissioners until after the next Congress convened in December of the following year; nor could they be on the scene before the spring of 1826. He further stated that since a period of one year would be required to make the survey, the boundary would remain undefined by treaty for two years. [8]

Alaman again on September 20, 1825, wished to ascertain the old boundary between the United States and Spanish possessions as defined by the treaty of 1795; he asked Poinsett to trace the line on Melish's Map. Poinsett did so with the observation that the treaty was concluded before the purchase of Louisiana by the United States from France in 1803. Upon inquiry as to why he wanted this information from Poinsett, Alaman observed that he thought it advisable to specify the old line in the proposed treaty until a new line could be agreed upon. Poinsett assured him that before the treaty between Spain and the United States of 1819 was concluded, the United States claimed the territory to the Rio Bravo del Norte while Spain claimed all territory west of the Mississippi River; that the treaty was a compromise which was binding upon the Mexican Government since the treaty was concluded before Mexican independence and since the accredited agents of the Mexican

6 Alaman to Poinsett, Mexico City, July 20, 1825, **ibid.**, pp. 20-21.

7 Poinsett to Alaman, Mexico City, July 18, 1825, **ibid.**, p. 19.

8 Poinsett to Alaman, Mexico City, July 27, 1825, **ibid.**, pp. 21-22.

Government in Washington had acknowledged its validity. Poinsett further stated that there had been ample time to have carried the treaty into effect but that the government of the United States had refrained from doing so only by motives of delicacy toward Mexico; that the same motive had induced him to propose a new treaty which should not allude to the Spanish treaty of 1819; but in so doing, he cautioned the Mexican minister that he did not intend to yield any territory within the limits of the United States as provided in the 1819 treaty. Poinsett thought that a more advantageous boundary might be drawn between the two countries, but that line must not be sought east of the Sabine or north of the Red and Arkansas rivers. He concluded the interview by stating that no article such as Alaman proposed could be inserted in the treaty without a renewal of the claim to all the territory north and east of the Rio Bravo by the United States.[9]

For the next few months the attention of the diplomats was turned from the question of boundaries to the formulation of a commercial treaty between Mexico and the United States. As the negotiations for the commercial treaty were nearing a conclusion on June 19, 1826, the Mexican representatives, S. Comachio and Jose' Ignacio Esteva, proposed an additional article declaring that the contracting parties should take into consideration the negotiation of a treaty of limits as soon as possible; that, in the meantime, the contracting parties pledge to assist the work of commissioners who might be sent by either power to examine the country near the proposed boundary. The article further proposed that unauthorized settlement by citizens of either country should not constitute valid claims to the land on which they settled.[10] By this proposal, the Mexican Government should have nullified any claim of the United States to the area south of the Red River which might be based upon the settlement of 200 families from the United States in that area.[11]

Poinsett accepted the article but he emphasized the fact that it was totally unnecessary because the United States considered the treaty of 1819 with Spain as binding upon Mexico. He was ready, however, to

9 Poinsett to Clay, Mexico City, September 20, 1825, **ibid.**, pp. 23-24.

10 Comachio and Esteva to Poinsett, Mexico City, June 19, 1826, **American State Papers, Foreign Relations**, Vol. VI, p. 599.

11 Charles Francis Adams, (ed.), **Memoirs of John Quincy Adams,** Vol. IV., pp. 266-269.

accede to the wishes of the Mexican Government in the matter if that government wished to designate a new boundary line which might serve to alleviate certain difficulties that, in his opinion, would certainly arise should the limits as agreed upon by the treaty of 1819 be allowed to stand.[12]

The determination of the Mexican Government to gain more information in regard to the area of the boundary line was reflected in the appointment of a Mexican commission under the leadership of General Don Mier Teran, with orders to start the survey by September, 1828.[13] Poinsett, in private conversation with the President of Mexico, attempted to convince him of the uselessness of the expedition until a treaty of limits should be definitely settled; the President replied that the public was anxious to have that question settled as soon as possible, and that in order to facilitate the accomplishment of this task, he had appointed Don Jose Ignacio Esteva and Don Juan Jose Espinosa as plenipotiaries to treat with the United States.[14] The plan of the Mexican Government to conclude the boundary question did not materialize because the money to defray the expenses of the commission under the leadership of General Teran was not made available until September 6, 1827.[15] On March 1, 1828, however, the commission arrived at Bexar ready to begin its work.[16]

By January 8, 1828, the Mexican Government had definitely decided to insist on the boundary line as provided in the treaty of 1819. When the commercial treaty, which had been signed on July 10, 1826, reached the Mexican Chamber of Deputies for ratification the following year, that chamber passed a resolution declaring that it would not ratify the treaty until an article should be inserted recognizing the validity of the Treaty

12 Poinsett to Comachio and Esteva, Mexico City, June 26, 1826, **American State Papers, Foreign Relations**, Vol. VI, p. 599.

13 Poinsett to Clay, Mexico City, July 12, 1826, **House Executive Documents, Twenty-fifth Congress, First Session** (Serial 311) Doc. No. 42, Vol. I, p. 24; Orland Morton, **Teran' and Texas, A Chapter in Texas-Mexico Relations,** pp. 42-82.

14 Poinsett to Clay, Mexico City, October 6, 1827, **ibid.**, pp. 25-26.
15 **Ibid.**

16 **Diary of the Expedition of the Frontiers of the Republic . . .Manuel de Mier y Teran et al.,** Archives, University of Texas Library.

of 1819 in regard to boundary limits. Poinsett agreed to the article but suggested that the question of limits and the commercial treaty should be discussed separately; with the assurance that negotiations on the boundary limits would proceed immediately, the Mexican Government agreed to this suggestion. [17]

In the beginning of the negotiations on the boundary question, Poinsett explained that the limits as provided by the Treaty of 1819, were liable to some objections and might be altered to benefit both parties; still, if the Mexican Government insisted upon the execution of articles three and four of that treaty, he would not object to it. He reminded them that any alteration of the treaty depended upon the mutual consent of both governments. [18] On January 10, 1828, both parties agreed upon the preamble of the treaty and incorporated the third and fourth articles of the Treaty of 1819 as a part of that agreement. [19] In order to effect a speedy conclusion of the question of limits, the contracting parties agreed that the treaty must be ratified by both the United States and the Mexican Governments within four months. [20]

The United States Senate promptly ratified the treaty but by delay on the part of the Mexican Secretary of State in presenting the treaty to the Mexican Congress for ratification, the four month limit expired before that body took action.[21] This delay consequently necessitated a reconsideration by the United States Senate. As the Congress had adjourned, nothing could be done until the following winter; by that time, the United States Senate was not sufficiently interested in the treaty to ratify it. In April of the following year, Jose M. Montoya, the

17 Poinsett to Clay, Mexico City, January 8, 1828, **House Executive Documents, Twenty-fifth Congress, First Session** (Serial 311) Doc. No. 42, Vol. I, p. 26.

18 **Ibid.,** p. 27

19 **Ibid.,** p. 26.

20 **American State Papers, Foreign Relations,** Vol. VI, pp. 946-947.

21 Pablo Obregon to Henry Clay, Washington, August 2, 1828, **House Executive Documents, Twenty-fifth Congress, First Session** (Serial 311) Doc. No. 42, Vol. I, p. 48; Brent to Obregon, Washington August 2, 1828, **ibid.,** p. 48.

Mexican charge d'affaires at Washington, brought the matter to the attention of the United States Government by saying that he presumed the treaty had been presented to the Senate, as he understood that would be necessary. He furthermore asked whether the Secretary of State was prepared to proceed with ratifications. [22] Exchange, however, was delayed for almost a year; by this time the United States had determined to seek negotiations for a new treaty of limits.

In order to revive the treaty of January 12, 1828, the time limit for ratification was extended on April 5, 1831, for one year. [23] The treaty was ratified by the Mexican Senate in October, 1831, [24] and was placed in the hands of Secretary of State Edward Livingston in February, 1832. The United States Senate took no immediate action on the treaty since it was evidently not anxious to ratify it. The Senate, however, was eager to conclude the commercial treaty which was pending at that time. The Mexican Government, on the contrary, was especially anxious for the United States Senate to rafity the treaty on limits. On March 31, 1832, Montoya informed the Secretary of State that he was prepared to exchange the treaty on commerce and navigation when the United States Government wished to exchange the treaty on limits. [9]

In response to this letter, Livingston informed Montoya that the Senate had ratified the commercial treaty but had not at that time considered the treaty on limits. This news distressed Montoya since only five days remained before the time limit would expire. [26] In order to hasten action by the United States Senate, Montoya informed Livingston that he positively would not exchange the commercial treaty, which the American Government desired so much, without the exchange of the treaty on limits which the Mexican Government valued so highly. [27] The

22 Montoya to Martin Van Buren, Washington, April 16, 1829, **ibid.**, p. 49.

23 Malloy, (ed.), **Treaties and Conventions**, Vol. I., pp. 1084-1085.

24 **House Executive Documents, Twenty-fifth Congress, Second Session** (Serial 332) Doc. No. 351, Vol. XII, pp. 407-408.

25 Montoya to Livingston, March 31, 1832, **Congressional Debates,** Vol. XIV, Pt. 2, App. 142.

26 Livingston to Montoya, March 31, 1832, **ibid.**, p. 142.

27 Montoya to Livingston, April 3, 1832, **ibid.**, p. 143.

United States Senate ratified the treaty on limits two days later after which the treaties were immediately exchanged. [28]

The Congress of the United States passed an act on July 3, 1832, providing for the appointment of a commissioner, surveyor, and clerk in accordance to the provisions of the treaty. [29] Edward Livingston informed Montoya of this act and inquired whether the Mexican Government had made similar arrangements for the survey of the boundary line as provided in the treaty of limits. If the Mexican Government had not done so, he suggested that Montoya urge his government to give immediate attention to the matter. [30] On November 29, 1832, Anthony Butler reminded the Mexican Government that the United States was prepared to carry out the provisions of the boundary treaty by appointing commissioners to survey the line. [31]

In December, 1833, Don Joaquin Maria de Costello y Lanzas, the new Mexican charge d'affaires at Washington, informed Secretary of State Louis McLane that Lieutenant Colonel Don Tomas Ramon del Morel had been appointed boundary commissioner and Don Costello Navarro had been selected as surveyor by the Mexican Government. He, at the same time, inquired whether the United States had made similar appointments.[32] When McLane inquired of Costello as to when the appointments were made, [33] Costello replied that he had not been advised on that point, but that the dispatch bore the date of September 25, 1833. He acknowledged the fact that the time for the appointments,

28 Malloy, (ed.), **Treaties and Conventions**, Vol. I, pp. 1084-1085.

29 Richard Peters, (ed.), **Public Statutes at Large of the United States of America**, 1789-1845, Vol. IV, p. 558, cited hereafter as Peters, (ed.), **Statutes at Large.**

30 Livingston to Montoya, Washington, July 20, 1832, **Congressional Debates**, Vol. XIV, p. 144.

31 Butler to Francisco Fagoaga, Washington, November 29, 1832, **House Executive Documents, Twenty-fifth Congress, Second Session** (Serial 332) Doc. No. 351, Vol. XII, pp. 459-460.

32 Costello to McLane, Washington, December 2, 1833, **ibid.**, pp. 60-61.

McLane to Costello, Washington, December 31, 1833, **Congressional Debates**, Vol. XIV, Pt. 2, App. 144.

as provided for in the treaty, had expired on April 5, 1833; and he attributed the delay to unsettled political conditions in Mexico. He further pledged the sincerity of the Mexican Government in its desire to fulfill its treaty obligations. [34]

McLane had learned from a report of the foreign minister to the Mexican Congress on May 20, 1833, that no commission had been appointed at that time. He therefore informed Butler that the treaty of limits could not be enforced until an extension of time would have been effected by a new convention. [35] Unfortunately, by a delay in transmittal, the dispatch did not reach Mexico City until June, 1834; [36] in the meantime, Costello reiterated the fact that the delay on the part of his government had been unavoidable; that the delay should not affect the enforcement of the treaty especially since the United States commissioners had not yet proceeded to the ground of operation. He assured McLane that power to extend the time limit in convention would be forwarded to him on June 1, 1834. [37] As these promised powers had not arrived on June 11, 1834, McLane authorized Butler to negotiate an additional article to the treaty in Mexico City, providing for an extension of time limit. [38]

The authority to negotiate which Costello expected by June 1, 1834, was not dispatched from Mexico City until October 21, 1834. [39] On December 4, Costello informed John Forsythe, the American Secretary of State, that the Mexican Government had appointed boundary

34 Costello to McLane, Washington, January 9, 1834, **House Executive Documents, Twenty-fifth Congress, First Session** (Serial 311) Doc. No. 42, Vol. I, pp. 61-62.

35 McLane to Butler, Washington, January 13, 1834, **Congressional Debates,** Vol. XIV, Pt. 2, App., pp. 130-131.

36 Butler to McLane, Mexico City, July 1, 1834, **ibid.,** pp. 130-131.

37 Costello to McLane, Washington, June 26, 1834, **ibid.,** pp. 144-145.

38 McLane to Butler, Washington, June 11, 1834, **House Executive Documents, Twenty-fifth Congress, Second Session** (Serial 332) Doc. No. 351, Vol. XII, pp. 142-143.

39 Francisco M. Lombardo to John Forsythe, October 21, 1834, **Congressional Debates,** Vol. XIV, Pt. 2, App., p. 145.

commissioners.[40] Forsythe replied that since time was so short until the Mexican Congress convened, and since he had authorized Butler to negotiate, he preferred to let him handle the matter at Mexico City.[41] Costello sensed a desire on the part of the American Government to procrastinate; he called Forsythe's attention to the fact that he had sent powers to negotiate to Butler in July, yet the Mexican Government had dispatched like powers to him almost four months later. This was evidence that Butler had not apprised the Mexican Government of that fact and that nothing was being done in Mexico City in regard to the extension of the treaty. As a further argument on the point, he pointed out that the United States Congress would adjourn six weeks earlier than the Mexican Congress, indicating that there would be a better chance of ratification by the Senates of both governments should the convention be ratified in Washington. [42]

Still hoping to conclude a new treaty of limits, Butler informed the Mexican Secretary of State that he had received authority to negotiate on the matter, and that he was anxious to conclude the treaty in time for it to be approved before the adjournment of the American Congress on the ensuing March 4.[43] In reply to this proposal, Gutierrez de Estrada, the Mexican Secretary of State, rejected the proposal on the ground that negotiations were in progress in Washington.[44]

Butler, consequently, dropped the matter until Estrada informed him on March 29, 1835, that nothing was being done in Washington in regard to the treaty on limits; that he and the Mexican Secretary of the Treasury had been empowered to treat with Butler on the matter. They encountered no difficulty in revising the treaty by which commissioners to survey the boundary line would be appointed within one year from

40 Costello to Forsythe, Washington, December 4, 1834, **ibid.**, p. 145.

41 Forsythe to Costello, Washington, December 11, 1834, **ibid.**, pp. 145-146.

42 Costello to Forsythe, Washington, January 12, 1835, **ibid.**, p. 147.

43 Butler to Lombardo, Mexico City, December 21, 1834, **ibid.**, p. 138.

44 Gutierrez de Estrada to Butler, Mexico City, February 7, 1835, **ibid.**, pp. 138-139.

April 3, 1835.[45] Ratifications were exchanged on April 20, 1836.

As Texas won its independence at this time, Mexico no longer had an interest in the boundary, [46] and consequently the boundary question became a problem concerning the United States and the Republic of Texas. Texas lost no time in revealing to the government of the United States its position in regard to the boundary line between the two countries. On November 18, 1836, William H. Wharton, the Texas minister plenipotentiary to the United States, was instructed to claim all the territory to the Rio Bravo del Norte for Texas. He was authorized to agree on a line which would begin at the mouth of the Rio Bravo del Norte on the Gulf of Mexico, proceed up the middle of that stream to its most northerly source; thence northward to the boundary which had been established by the Florida treaty of 1819 between Spain and the United States at the head of the Arkansas River; thence along that line to the mouth of the Sabine River. The instructions correctly stated that the treaty of 1819 established the line along the south bank of the Arkansas River but erroneously stated that the line was along the south bank of Red River and along the middle of the Sabine River. Wharton was instructed to secure the middle of all the streams as the boundary line in order that Texas might control landings and ferries. In event that he should not be able to effect this change, his instructions stated that control of the bank on the Texas side to low water would suffice. [47]

In accordance with these instructions, Wharton informed Secretary of State John Forsythe that the Texas Government expected to have the boundary settled according to the Spanish treaty of 1819.[48] Pursuing the question further, this boundary line was defined by the Texas Congress in an act of June 12, 1837, which further provided that the President of Texas negotiate with the United States Government in regard to the

45 Costello to Ashbury Dickens, Washington, June 2, 1835, **ibid.**, pp. 147-148.

46 Malloy, (ed.), **Treaties and Conventions**, Vol. I, p. 1099.

47 Stephen F. Austin to Wharton, Washington, November 18, 1836, George P. Garrison, (ed.), "Diplomatic Correspondence of the Republic of Texas." Vol. II, pp. 127-134, in the **American Historical Association Reports, 1908**; cited hereafter as Garrison, (ed.), **Diplomatic Correspondence of the Republic of Texas.**

48 Austin to Wharton, Washington, January 11, 1837, **ibid.**, p. 179.

survey of the boundary as had been agreed upon by the treaty of 1819. [49]

The attention of the diplomats was then turned to Northeast Texas by the establishment of a land district with headquarters at George Wright's house which was situated in present Red River County. [50] Forsythe vigorously protested against this act since the area was situated in the region which could fall within the bounds of the United States when the boundary line should be established. [51] This protest prompted President Sam Houston to call a special session of the Congress to consider the boundary question. He informed the members that he had not appointed a commissioner to survey the line as was provided for in the act of June 12, 1837, [52] because the Government of the United States had not made provision for a commissioner. [53] In response to this message, Congress provided for the appointment of a commissioner to survey the line from the mouth of the Sabine River to the intersection of the 100th meridian with Red River according to the treaty between the United States and Mexico in 1828. [54] Before this law could be executed, however, a new dispute arose by the creation of Red River County by the Texas government on December 18, 1837. [55] After a

49 **Laws of the Republic of Texas**, Vol. I, p. 133.

50 **Ibid.**, pp. 216-224.

51 Forsythe to Catlett, Washington, June 17, 1837, Garrison, (ed.), **Diplomatic Correspondence of the Republic of Texas**, Vol. II, p. 230.

52 **Laws of the Republic of Texas**, Vol. I, p. 133.

53 **House Journal, Texas Congress, Called Session**, beginning on September 25, 1837, and **Regular Session**, beginning November 6, 1837, pp. 15-17.

54 Garrison, (ed.), **Diplomatic Correspondence of the Republic of Texas**, Vol. II, pp. 196-197.

55 **Secret Journal of the [Texas] Senate**, pp. 92-93; **Law of the Republic of Texas**, Vol. II, p. 89.

heated dispute over the boundary line of northeast Texas, [56] Robert A. Irion instructed Memucan Hunt to negotiate the whole question of boundaries; Irion favored the survey of the line between 32nd degree north latitude and Red River, but he specifically expressed his opposition to the survey of the line along 100th meridian on the ground that the country was infested by hostile Indians and that an unnecessary expense would be incurred by the necessity of maintaining an armed force for the protection of the surveyors. [57]

He was especially concerned over the possibility that the United States might insist on the survey of the entire boundary line; on March 21, he wrote a second letter to Hunt in which he confessed that if the United States should insist on running the entire line, he was not in a position to instruct Hunt since the Texas Congress had provided for the line to be run only to the 100th meridian. [58]

When Hunt received his full powers to negotiate a boundary treaty on April 13, 1838, he encountered little difficulty in reaching an agreement with the United States Government. The boundary line delineated in the treaty between the United States and Spain in 1819 was accepted. The treaty further provided that each government would appoint a commissioner and a surveyor who would meet within a year after the exchange of ratifications for the purpose of surveying the boundary line from the mouth of the Sabine River to the Red River. It was further provided that the remainder of the line would be surveyed at the convenience of both governments. [59]

56 La Branche to Irion, Houston, January 15, 1838, Garrison, (ed.), **Diplomatic Correspondence of the Republic of Texas**, Vol. II, p. 282; Irion to La Branche, Houston, January 16, 1838, **ibid.**, Vol. II, p. 282; La Branche to Irion, Houston, January 16, 1838, **ibid.**, p. 283; Irion to La Branche, Houston, February 13, 1838, **ibid.**, pp. 298-310; La Branche to Irion, Washington (Texas), March 3, 1838, **ibid.**, pp. 310-312; Hunt to Forsythe, Washington (Texas), March 8, 1838, **ibid.**, p. 315) Forsythe to Hunt, Washington (Texas), March 9, 1838, **ibid.**, p. 318.

57 Irion to Hunt, Houston, March 21, 1838, **ibid.**, p. 318.

58 **Ibid.**, pp. 320-321.

59 **House Documents, Twenty-fifth Congress, Third Session** (Serial 344) Doc. No. 2, Vol. II, 34; Malloy, (ed.), **Treaties and Conventions**, Vol. II, pp. 1779-1780.

CHAPTER III

Geography Of The Region 1803-1852

The people of the United States knew neither how much territory they had gained by the purchase of Louisiana, nor what sort of country they had acquired. A congressman gave a vivid picture of their lack of knowledge when he said: "The masses of virgin gold and silver that glitter in the veins and rocks which underlie the Arkansas River mingle with the minerals near certain other streams and offer themselves to the hand of him who will gather, refine and convert them to use are common and wonderful.[1]"

Philip Nolan explored a part of Texas in 1800; Ellis P. Bean, in giving an account of this expedition, stated that a band of Comanche Indians numbering about 200 visited Nolan's party. Bean concluded by saying: "We went with them to the South Fork of Red River to see their chief by the name of Nicoraco where we stayed with them a month."[2] This is the first indication that there was more than one branch of upper Red River. Further information is lacking since Bean neither mentioned the North Fork nor did he leave a map of the country.

President Thomas Jefferson early evinced an interest in Louisiana in 1804 when he authorized Meriwether Lewis and William Clark to explore this region. In their report, they referred to the Pawnee Indians who lived on the "Upper Red River." The expedition threw little additional light on the upper reaches of Red River except by a map which extended as far south as the 33rd degree of north latitude. This map, which delineates only the upper part of Red River, shows only one

1 **Annals of Congress, Eighth Congress, First Session,** (Serial X13) Vol. I, p. 1126.

2 W.P. Yoakum (ed.), **Memoirs of Ellis P. Bean,** p. 16; Henderson K. Yoakum, **History of Texas,** Vol. I, p. 404-405.

stream which rises in the vicinity of the 35th degree north latitude and 105th degree west longitude; the river is shown to flow southeastward to the region of 101st degree west longitude and 33 degrees north latitude.[3]

The President was especially interested in determining the nature of the Red River valley. He called upon William C.C. Claiborne, the Governor of Louisiana; Daniel Clark, the former United States Consul at New Orleans; and William Dunbar, the noted scientist of the lower Mississippi Valley, for information in regard to the country. Claiborne called upon Dr. John Sibley, who was acting Indian agent at Natchitoches, for assistance in the project. Sibley made two reports to the Secretary of War, the first of which was prepared on April 5, 1805. This report contained an account of the Indian tribes in that area. The second report, which was published in 1810, described the country adjacent to Red River. Upon these two documents rested the available geographical information of Red River until Pike published his map in 1816.[4]

Jefferson planned to send an expedition up Red River to its source, across to the headwaters of the Arkansas River and down that stream to its mouth. He asked Dunbar to direct this project provided he should be successful in inducing Congress to provide the funds. When Congress appropriated 3,000 dollars for the purpose, he again asked Dunbar to supervise the preparations to select the leaders.[5] In the meantime, Dr. George Hunter, acting under the orders of the Secretary of War, was in Philadelphia purchasing provisions, Indian presents, medicines, and instruments for the expedition; who then proceeded to Pittsburg, where he supervised the construction of a flat-bottom boat with which to transport the supplies to Natchez.

When he arrived at Natchez two months later, he found that Lieutenant Colonel Constant Freeman, commander of the garrison at New Orleans, who was to furnish the boat and supply the escort, had awaited his arrival to start preparations. Before these preparations could be

3 **Annals of Congress, Ninth Congress, Second Session** (serial X16) Vol. II, pp. 1035-1041.

4 **House Executive Documents, Fifty-eighth Congress, Third Session** (Serial 4884) Doc. No. 429, CCV, 151-174; William C.C. Claiborne to John Sibley, New Orleans, June 10, 1805, Dunbar Rowland, (ed.), **Letters of William C.C. Claiborne**, Vol. III, p. 87.

5 **House Documents, Fifty-eighth Congress, Third Session** (Serial 4884) Doc. No. 429, CCV, pp. 151-174.

completed, however, defection among the Osage Indians made it impractical to send the expedition into the Indian country adjacent to Red River. [6]

In the meantime, Congress voted an additional 5,000 dollars for the exploration of Red River. After consideration of several men for the leadership of the proposed expedition, Hunter selected Thomas Freeman to command the force with Lieutenant William Humphrey as his assistant, and Dr. Peter Curtis as the official botanist. As the result of experience gained in transporting baggage over land by Dunbar's expedition, Freeman was ordered to proceed to the source of Red River and to return by the same route. Governor Claiborne applied to the Marquis of Casa Calvo for passports for the members of Freeman's party. Casa Calvo complied, but he added that since the source of Red River was likely within the territory of Spain, he would give due notice to Captain General Don Nemesio Salcedo in order that he might take such measures as the situation demanded. [8]

Casa Calvo informed Salcedo that he had issued the passports, and that he had left him to do whatever he thought was necessary in regard to the matter. In Salcedo's reply, he informed Casa Calvo that although the expedition bore his passport, Salcedo, as Captain General, understood the interests of his government better than did Casa Calvo, and that he would protect those interests against the proposed expedition. Salcedo immediately ordered the governor of Texas to dispatch a military force to intercept Freeman. [9]

Freeman expected to ascend the river in boats to the country of the Pawnee Indians; here it was his intention to leave the boats and after packing supplies on horses, which he expected to purchase from these Indians, Freeman intended to proceed to the source of the river at the

6 To make use of the men and supplies, and to gain experience in the technique of exploring, President Jefferson authorized Dunbar to lead the expedition up the Washita River as far as present Hot Springs, **ibid.**, pp. 151-174.

8 Casa Calvo had been governor of Louisiana; had come to Louisiana the second time to act as commissioner of Spain to transfer the territory to France; and after its transfer to the United States by France, had remained as a commissioner to assist in making the boundary between United States territory and Spanish territory. **Ibid.**

9 **Ibid.**

top of the mountains which he conjectured would be located about 500 miles away. The party encountered many difficulties and obstructions in the struggle up the river through the bayous and around a tremendous raft which was later known as the "Great Raft." The members had no more than overcome these formidable obstacles when they were met by an overwhelming force of Spanish cavalry near Spanish Bluffs, situated eight miles north of DeKalb, Texas, in Little River County, Arkansas. As the Spanish commander assured Freeman that he would resort to force in order to impede the further advance of his party, Freeman reluctantly retraced his steps to Natchitoches. [10]

While Freeman and Custis were trying to reach the source of Red River from Natchitoches in 1806, Lieutenant Zebulon Pike was ordered to ascend the Arkansas River to its source, strike across the country southward to the headwaters of Red River and descend that river to Natchitoches. After enduring many privations and intense sufferings from the deep snow in the lofty mountains about the source of the Arkansas River, Pike arrived upon a stream running to the east which he concluded was Red River, but which subsequently proved to be the Rio Grande. There, he was seized by the governor of New Mexico and sent home by way of Chihuahua and San Antonio. General James Wilkinson, under whose orders Pike was serving at the time, stated in a letter to him after his return as follows: "The principal object of your expedition up the Arkansas River was to discover the true position of the source of the Red River; this was not accomplished."[11]

Pike did, however, from the most accurate information which he could obtain, draw a map and a chart of the Red River region. Pike delineated Red River as extending from a point near Santa Fe between 27 degrees and 38 degrees north latitude to the mouth of the river in Louisiana. Both map and chart show a chain of mountains running north and south; the map indicates them as "White snow capped mountains, very high." There are two small streams east of the mountains labeled "Rio Rojo" and "Rio Moro," the source of the "Rio Rojo" being located northeast, that of the "Rio Moro" almost east of Santa Fe. The "Rio Rojo" rises between the 37 and 38 degrees north latitude while the "Rio Moro" rises between 36 and 37 degrees north latitude. The area between these prongs is marked, "Source of Red River of the Mississippi." These streams unite in the vicinity of the 37 degree north latitude to form one

10 **Senate Documents, Thirty-second Congress, Second Session** (Serial 666) Doc. No. 54, Vol. VIII, p. 1.

11 **Ibid.**

stream which is shown on the chart as "Red River" and on the map as "Rio Colorado of Natchitoches." Thus united, the channel runs for a short distance eastwardly and then southeastwardly until it reaches a point slightly west of the 100th meridian; then southeastwardly until it passes Natchitoches.[12] Pike was correct in the location of Rio Moro and Rio Rojo east of Santa Fe; these streams are headwaters of the North Canadian River, however, and not headwaters of the Red River as Pike thought.

The map which Humboldt published in 1811 is surprisingly correct in regard to the source of Red River. The "Quireches," as is shown on his map, has its source at 36 degrees north latitude and 100 degrees west longitude and runs in a southeastward direction to the 99th degree west longitude where it forms a junction with the "Natchitoches," which has its source at 36 degrees north latitude and 102 degrees and 30 minutes west longitude. The river formed by the confluence of these two streams labeled "River Rouge" continues in an eastward direction for some distance and then bears to the southeast. Like the maps which were published at an earlier date, the main stream shows few tributaries.[13]

On his map of 1816, William Darby indicated that upper Red River was formed by the junction of two prongs, after which it extended southeast-wardly from a point near the intersection of the 40th degree north latitude and the 107th degree west longitude "To the waters near the Mississippi." The unnamed streams which flow from the northwest are found east of 100 degree west longitude, each of which is much shorter than the main Red River as is delineated on the map. Darby stated that Red River rises 30 or 40 miles east of Santa Fe in the vicinity of the intersection of 37 degrees north latitude and 107 degrees west longitude,

12 **Account of Expedition to the Source of the Mississippi and through the Western parts of Louisiana to the Source of the ARkansas, La Platte, Pierre and San Juan Rivers, Performed by Order of the Government of the United States Government During the Years 1805, 1806, 1807; and a Tour Through the Interior Parts of New Spain When Conducted Through These Provinces by Order of the Captain General in the Year 1807**, pp. 44-47.

13 Alexander De Humboldt, **Political Essay on the Kingdom of New Spain**, Vol. I, p. 1.

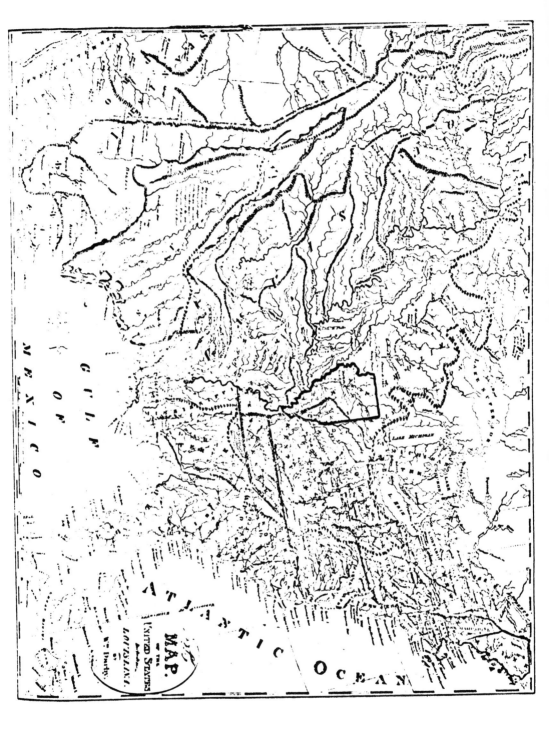

and that it pursued a southeast course for 450 miles.[14] Darby, like Pike, confused the headwaters of the Canadian River with those of the Red River.

Melish, like his predecessors, had not actually explored the country in preparation of his map; he used Pike's work as a source.[15] The Red River, according to this map and the description of Melish, is a single stream rising in the mountains east of Santa Fe between 37 and 38 degrees north latitude and pursuing a general southeast course, making several remarkable bends but having no important tributaries until it forms a junction with the Ouachita River between 96 and 97 degrees west longitude.[16]

Major Stephen H. Long began his expedition into the West from Pittsburg on May 3, 1819, only a few months after the Treaty of 1819 between Spain and the United States was signed. The instructions to him, given by Secretary of War John C. Calhoun indicate that the purpose of the expedition was to explore the country between the Mississippi River and the Rocky Mountains, by first exploring the Missouri River and its tributaries and then in succession, the Red, the Arkansas, and the Mississippi rivers above the mouth of the Missouri River.

Long was able to carry out these instructions only in part; he explored the Missouri and its tributaries as far north as the Platte River. Following that stream to the Rocky Mountains, he turned southward and explored the upper reaches of the Arkansas River. Moving again southward, he came to a stream which he judged to be Red River; as he descended the stream to the point where it emptied into the Arkansas River, he found, to his disappointment, that this was the Canadian River instead of the Red.[17] In reporting this part of the expedition, Major

14 William Darby, **A Geographical Description of the State of Louisiana, Being Accompanied by the Map of Louisiana,** pp. 51-53. (Painted for the author and published by John Melish, Philadelphia, 1816.)

15 John Melish, **A Geographical Description of the United States with the Contiguous British and Spanish Possessions Intended as an Accompaniment to Melish's Map of These Countries,** p. 9.

16 **Ibid.,** pp. 11-12.

17 Stephen H. Long, **An Expedition from Pittsburg to the Rocky Mountains,** Vol. I, pp. 3-4.

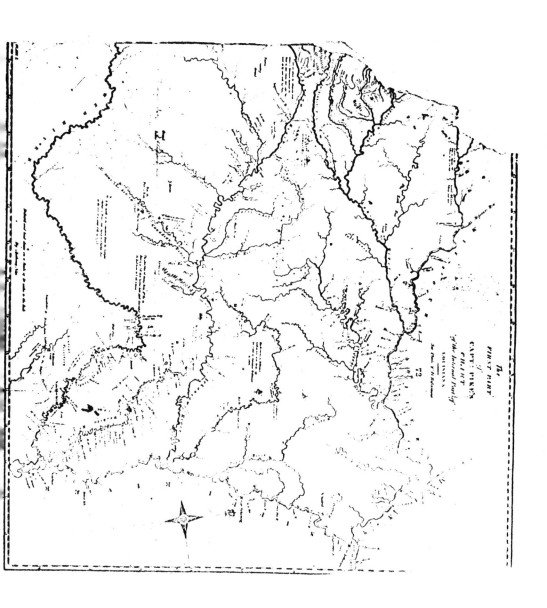

The
FIRST PART
of
CAPT. PIKE'S
CHART
of the Internal Part of
LOUISIANA
See Plate N°II. Reference

Long said that he arrived at a creek having a westwardly course which he thought to be a tributary of Red River. He descended this stream for 200 miles where a band of Bad Heart Indians assured him that the stream was Red River. He continued his march down the river for several hundred miles to discover that the stream was the Canadian River. [18]

Edwin James, botanist and geographer of the expedition, summed up the results of Long's explorations in the following words: "We are as yet ignorant of the true position of the sources of Red River." James further stated that the upper Canadian was the Red River of Pike, Darby, and Humboldt, which had been generally mistaken for the source of Red River of Natchitoches. He suggested that since the water of all the rivers in the area was red, it was not surprising that several rivers might have received the same name. [19]

This similarity of streams and the reliance upon Pike as an authority may account for the general mistake of later geographers in the belief that Rio Oro and Rio Mora, headwaters of the North Fork of the Canadian River, were the headwaters of the Red River. John H. Robinson published a map in 1819 on which he located the headwaters of Red River in the vicinity of Santa Fe. [20] H.C. Carey and James Lea published an atlas in 1822 in which they delineated the headwaters of Red River east of Santa Fe. [21] Although Robinson, Carey, and Lea published their maps before the correct analysis of James was published in 1823, geographers continued to follow Pike's theory that the source of Red River was in the vicinity of Santa Fe.

Interest in Red River on the part of Texas was demonstrated in 1840 by the establishment of a military and supply post by William G. Cooke

18 **Ibid.**, Vol. II, p. 216.

19 **Ibid.**, Vol. II, p. 216.

20 John H. Robinson, **A Map of Mexico, Louisiana, and Missouri Territory, Including the States of Mississippi, Alabama Territory, East and West Florida, Georgia, South Carolina, and Part of the Island of Cuba.** (A copy of this map is in the Archives, University of Texas.)

21 H.C. Carey and James Lea, **The Geography, History, and Statistics of America, and the West Indies**, p. 1.

eleven miles above Coffee's trading house.[22] The Texas-Santa Fe Expedition under the command of Hugh McLeod left Bushy Creek, located about twenty miles north of Austin, for Santa Fe in June, 1842. The expedition planned to move northward to Red River and follow the south side of that river toward Santa Fe. The party turned westward along a stream which it thought was Red River, but the stream proved to be the Wichita River. When the expedition became lost in a rough, arid country, McLeod sent a detachment northward in search of Santa Fe. This party succeeded in reaching Mora on the headwaters of the Canadian River.

George Wilkins Kendall, who was a member of the Texas-Santa Fe Expedition, observed that the map makers had erroneously extended the upper course of Red River 200 or 300 miles too far west; he correctly concluded that the Mora was a source of the Canadian River and that the source of Red River was located north of the headwaters of the Brazos and the Colorado rivers. Kendall correctly concluded that the Red River of the United States had been traced and was well known to a point west of Coffee's trading post located west of the mouth of the Washita River; that beyond that point, it lost itself in speculation and that it would never be known until it should be explored to its source. [23]

In 1843 the Texas Government granted Major Jacob Snively permission to intercept Mexican traders on the Santa Fe Trail in the vicinity of the Arkansas River. Snively with 180 men set out from Georgetown in Fannin Country Texas on April 25, 1843. He reported that he marched along the south side of Red River a distance of 150 miles. As Snively's chief interest was not in geography, he added little to information in regard to Red River.[24]

A map compiled for the Department of State under the direction of Colonel J.W. Abert and Lieutenant W.H. Emory in 1844 shows Red River as running westward to the 10th meridian; the course of the river

22 William G. Cooke to Branch T. Archer, Camp on Bois d'arc, November 14, 1840, Army Papers, 1840-1846, Archives, Texas State Library.

23 George Wilkins Kendall, **Narrative of the Texas-Santa Fe Expedition,** Vol. I, pp. 218, 249-250.

24 M.C. Hamilton to Major Jacob Snively, Austin, February 13, 1843, Army Papers, 1840-1846, Archives, Texas State Library); Snively to Hamilton, Clarksville, July 9, 1843, **ibid.**

then turns northwestward to a point near Santa Fe. [25] On his map of 1848, J.H. Colton shows that Red River forks at the 98th meridian: one fork of which extends northwestwardly toward Santa Fe, marked "Rio Roxo or Red River," between 100 degrees and 102 degrees west longitude, and "Red River" between 102 degrees and 104 degrees.[26] Edward Smith further demonstrated the lack of information in regard to the source of Red River when he published a map in 1849 on which he shows the headwaters of Red River a short distance east of Santa Fe. [27]

While Captain Randolph B. Marcy was exploring the regions lying upon the Canadian, the Arkansas, the Trinity, the Brazos, and the Colorado rivers between 1849 and 1852, his attention was called to the remarkable fact that a portion of one of the largest and most important rivers in the United States, situated directly within the area which he had been examining, remained unexplored and unknown. No white man had ever ascended Red River to its source; the only information available was derived from the meager facts which Pike had gathered, from the Indians, and from semi-civilized traders. This of course was unreliable, indefinite, and unsatisfactory. [28]

In the spring of 1852, the Government of the United States ordered Marcy to make an exploration of the region. Accompanied by Captain George B. McClellan of the army engineers, he crossed Red River below the mouth of the Big Wichita River and proceeded up the north side of Red River, striking the North Fork near the mouth of Otter Creek. Marcy then established the point of intersection of the 100th meridian with Red River; this point fell about six miles below the point of confluence of the North Fork and the South Fork. He then ascended the North Fork to its source, which was located on the intersection of 101 degrees and 55 minutes west longitude with 35 degrees and 35 minutes north latitude. From that point, Marcy moved southward in search of the South Fork or Prairie Dog Town River as the Indians called it. He at

25 **House Documents, Twenty-eighth Congress, Second Session** (Serial 463), Doc. No. 15, Vol. I, p. 45.

26 J.H. Colton **Map of California, Oregon, and Texas, 1847,** (Copy in Archives, University of Texas.)

27 Edward Smith, **Account of a Journey Through Northeastern Texas Undertaken in 1849 for the Purposes of Emigration,** p. 1.

28 Randolpy B. Marcy, **Explorations of Red River of Louisiana,** pp. 1-12.

length found the source of the intersection of 34 degrees and 42 minutes north latitude with 103 degrees and 7 minutes west longitude.[29]

This expedition thus established the fact that the true 100th meridian was located about 80 miles west of the 100th meridian on the Melish Map, and that there were two forks of Upper Red River, the southern branch rising on the Llano Estacado and the other rising about 75 miles north of that point. This extended territory which lies between the two streams created the question of whether this area belonged to the state of Texas or to the United States. The answer could be found only by the location of the 100th meridian and by the determination of which fork of Red River would be considered as the boundary line according to the treaty of February 22, 1819, between the United States and Spain.

In order to acquire a true perspective of the problem concerning the boundary which divided the United States territory from Spanish territory which subsequently became territory of the state of Texas, the following portion of the treaty of 1819 must be kept in mind:

The boundary line between the two countries, west of the Mississippi, shall begin on the Gulf of Mexico, at the mouth of the River Sabine, in the Sea; continuing north along the western bank of that river, to the thirty-second degree of latitude; thence by a line due north, to the degree of latitude where it strikes the Rio Roxo of Natchitoches or Red River, thence following the course of the Rio Roxo westward to the degree of longitude one-hundred west from London, and twenty-three from Washington; then crossing said Red River, and running thence, by a line due north, to the River Arkansas; thence, following the course of the southern bank of the Arkansas to its source, in latitude forty-two degrees north; and thence by that parallel of latitude to the South Sea; the whole being laid down in Melish's Map of the United States, published at Philadelphia, Improved to the First of January 1818.[30]

Although the resolution by which the Congress of Texas accepted the proposal of the United States Congress to annex Texas did not mention boundaries, the Texas State Legislature did, on April 29, 1846, pass a resolution declaring exclusive right to the jurisdiction over the soil included in the late republic excepting such jurisdiction as was vested in the United States by the constitution of the United States and the general resolution of annexation, subject to such regulations and

29 **Ibid.**, p. 47.

30 **American State Papers, Foreign Relations,** Vol. IV, pp. 623-625.

controls which the United States Government might deem expedient.[32]

At this time, Texas comprised parts of the territory now included in the states of New Mexico, Oklahoma, Kansas, Colorado, and Wyoming. By an act of the United States Congress which was approved on September 9, 1850, the United States proposed to fix the eastern boundary of the Panhandle of Texas along the true 100th meridian from the Red River to 36 degrees and 30 minutes north latitude. It was further provided that "The State of Texas cedes to the United States all its claims to territory exterior to the limits and borders which it agrees to establish by the first article of this agreement." In return, Texas would relinquish all claims upon the United States for liability of debts and for compensation for the surrender to the United States for ships, forts, arsenals, custom houses, arms and ammunition of war, and public buildings which became the property of the United States at the time of annexation. In conclusion, it was proposed that "The United States in consideration of said establishment of boundaries, cession of claims to territory and relinquishment of other claims, will pay to the State of Texas the sum of 10,000,000 dollars."[33] The Legislature of Texas, by an act approved on November 25, 1850, agreed to the proposal,[34] and on December 13, 1850, President Millard Fillmore declared the act to be in effect.[35]

32 G.W. Paschal, (ed.), **A Digest of the Laws of Texas**, Vol. I, pp. 192-194.

33 George Minot, (ed.), **Statutes at Large**, Vol. IX, p. 446.

34 **Ibid.**, p. 1005.

35 **Ibid.**

CHAPTER IV

Surveys Of The One Hundredth Meridian

Not until Marcy's reconnaissance in 1852, which revealed not only the 100th meridian of the Melish Map was far east of the true meridian but that there were two forks of Red River, did the people of either the United States or Texas realize the tremendous importance of that part of this agreement which supplanted the part of article three in the treaty of 1819 which established the boundary line along the 100th meridian according to Melish's Map for the provision which placed the line along the true 100th meridian. In the hope, therefore, of removing the uncertainty of this question, the Texas Legislature passed an act on February 11, 1854, authorizing the appointment of a commissioner, surveyor, and a clerk to act in conjunction with such officers as might be appointed by the United States Government to run and mark the boundary line between the State of Texas and the territories of the United States from the point where it leaves the Red River to the point where it intersects the Rio Grande. The act further provided that such appointment would not be made until the United States Congress had authorized such officers.[1]

Although no immediate action was taken by the United States in regard to this matter, a treaty was made between the United States and the Choctaw and Chickasaw Indians in 1855 which defined the boundary of these Indian lands as beginning at a point on the Arkansas River 100 paces east of old Fort Smith where the western boundary line of the State of Arkansas crossed that river; thence up Red River to the point where the 100th. meridian intersects it; thence north along this meridian to the main Canadian River; thence down this river to its confluence with the Arkansas River and thence down the Arkansas to the point of beginning.[2] As that part of the boundary line from Red River to the

1 Charles Steward (ed.), **Laws of Texas, Fifth Legislature**, 1853, Vol. XIV, p. 81; H.P.N. Gammel (ed.), **Laws of Texas**, Vol. III, p. 1225.

2 George P. Sanger (ed.), **Statutes at Large**, Vol. XI, pp. 611-612.

Canadian River was also the boundary line between the State of Texas and territory of the United States, it was imperative that the line be established.

The Commissioner of Indian Affairs, therefore, employed Major A.H. Jones and Major H.M.C. Brown not only to survey the Indian lands but to mark and establish the boundary line.[3] The surveyors began their work in 1857 by establishing the initial monument on the 100th meridian 30 chains north of the South Fork of Red River. From that point, they surveyed northward to a point located nineteen miles north of the Canadian River.[4] In regard to the relative size of the branches of Red River, they reported in their field notes that the South Fork south of the initial monument was 76 chains and 85 links wide from high water mark to high water mark while the North Fork was 23 chains wide.[5] They therefore concluded that the South Fork was the channel of Red River.[6] The most significant result of this survey, however, was the establishment of the 100th meridian 80 miles west of Marcy's line and 74 miles west of the confluence of the North Fork with the South Fork of Red River, and that the determination as to which of these two streams was the Red River of the Melish map would establish the ownership of that vast area of land lying between the two rivers from north to south, and from their confluence on the east to the 100th meridian on the west.[7]

In the meantime, the Texas Senators and Representatives in Congress were urging the United States to appoint commissioners who, in

3 **Ibid., House Executive Documents, Fifty-seventh Congress**, First Session (Serial 4369) Doc. No. 635, Vol. CCII, pp. 12-14.

4 **House Documents, Forty-seventh Congress, First Session** (Serial 2069) Doc. No. 1282, Vol. V, pp. 4-5.

5 **House Documents, Fifty-seventh Congress, First Session** (Serial 4369) Doc. No. 635, CCII, 12-14.

6 As that part of the boundary line between the state of Texas and United States territory which extended from Jones and Brown's final monument to the point of intersection of 100th meridian with the line of thirty-six degrees and thirty minutes north latitude did not touch the Indian lands, Jones and Brown did not survey it.

7 **House Reports, Forty-seventh Congress, First Session** (Serial 2069) Doc. No. 1282, Vol. V, pp. 4-5.

cooperation with commissioners authorized by the Texas Legislature in 1854, to survey the 100th meridian. Representative P.H. Bell notified William L. Marcy, Secretary of State, that the Texas Legislature had passed the bill; he urged that a like provision be made on the part of the United States.[8] As Marcy did nothing in regard to the matter, Bell, on January 15, 1855, forwarded a copy of the letter to Robert McClelland, Secretary of Interior, with a request that he recommend the passage of a bill.[9] No record has been found in regard to McClelland's action concerning the request. President Franklin Pierce, however, in his message to Congress on March 1, 1855, recommended that provision be made to act in conjunction with the State of Texas for running the line.[10]

Nothing was done, however, until 1858, at which time Congress passed an act providing for a joint commission whose purpose it was to run and mark the boundary beginning at the point where the 100th degree west longitude crossed Red River, and running hence north to the point where the 100th degree intersects 36 degrees and 30 minutes north latitude; thence to the point where that parallel intersects the 103th degree west longitude; thence along that parallel to the 32nd degree north latitude; and thence west along that the 32nd parallel to the Rio Grande. It was further provided that landmarks be established at the point of beginning on Red River and at such other points as the joint commission might decide.[11]

In response to a letter from Secretary of Interior Jacob Thomas, informing him of this action by Congress,[12] Governor H.R. Runnels sent a message to the Texas Legislature on January 26, 1858, informing it of this action and recommending the adoption of necessary measures for the appointment of a commission to act with the proposed commission of

8 P.H. Bell to William L. Marcy, Washington, January 4, 1855, **House Executive Documents, Thirty-third Congress, Second Session** [Serial 790) Doc. No. 89, Vol. X, pp. 1-2.

9 P.H. Bell to Robert McClelland, Washington, January 15, 1855, **ibid.**

10 **Ibid.**

11 George P. Sanger (ed.), **Statutes at Large**, Vol. XI, p. 310.

12 Jacob Thompson to Governor H.R. Runnels, Washington, January 20, 1858, "Runnels Papers," Texas State Library.

the United States.[13]

Displaying an eagerness to settle the qustion of boundary and willingness to cooperate with the United States Government, the Texas Legislature passed an act providing for the running and marking the boundary line between the State of Texas and the territories of the United States.[14] Governor Runnels thereupon appointed William R. Scurry as commissioner, Charles B. Snowden as surveyor, and William A. Bush as secretary of the commission on the part of the State of Texas.[15]

According to the provisions of the act by the United States Congress, the Secretary of Interior was made responsible for the enforcement of its provisions. Therefore on July 9, 1858, he appointed John C. Clark as commissioner, surveyor, and astronomer to represent the United States on the joint commission. He instructed Clark to begin the survey on the Rio Grande at the point of intersection with the thirty second degree north latitude; following that latitude to the 103rd degree west longitude; from there the commission was to determine and mark the line along the 103rd degree northward to its intersection with the line along 36 degrees and 30 minutes north latitude. The instructions further provided that the commission take the point of intersection of the 36 degree and 30 minutes north latitude line with the 100th meridian line as was established by Jones and Brown, or as the commission might determine, and mark the line along the 100th meridian to Red River.[16]

In conclusion, Secretary Thompson stated that a duplicate copy of the instructions would be sent to the Governor of Texas for his information and concurrence. He cautioned Clark, however, that if the person designated to cooperate with him on the part of the State of Texas

13 Message from Governor H.R. Runnels to the Legislature of Texas, January 26, 1858, **ibid.**

14 As far as the writer has been able to find, there was no law approved of February 2, 1856, pertaining to this subject; there was such a law approved on February 11, 1854. H.P.N. Gammel (ed.), **General Laws of the State of Texas, 1854-1861**, p. 64; Charles Stewart (ed.), **Laws of Texas, Fifth Legislature, 1853**, Vol. XIV, p. 81.

15 Commissions may be found in State Department Boundary papers, 1837-1911, Texas State Library. Archives.

16 **Senate Documents, Forty-seventh Congress, First Session** (Serial 2076) Doc. No. 70, Vol. III, pp. 264-265.

should receive instructions from the proper authorities conflicting materially with this plan of operation, he might adopt any plan as might be mutually agreed upon provided it did not conflict with the interest of the United States.[17]

When Governor Runnels received a copy of these instructions, he replied on July 28, 1858, that he preferred to start the survey at the point where the 100th meridian crossed Red River as was provided for by the law which authorized the commission. He gave as his reason for starting the survey at that point, the fact that the people of Texas who lived and owned property in the disputed area were pressing for an immediate settlement of the boundary question.[18] In a reply on August 1, 1858, Secretary Thompson stated two major reasons for following his proposal; he was particularly interested in the saving of time and in the economy involved since each government would save 20,000 dollars by the acceptance of the line as was established by Jones and Brown along the 100th meridian in 1857.[19] There the question remained until Clark arrived in Austin on September 1, 1858. He met Governor Runnels who accompanied him to San Antonio, where they conferred with the Texas commissioner, William R. Scurry. As to the outcome of the conference, Clark reported to Thompson on September 8, 1858, that "They have concluded to adopt our plan throughout".[20]

The commissioners directed their efforts in surveying the southern and western boundaries of Texas until they retired to winter quarters in October, 1859. In a report by W.A. Bush of the Texas commission to Governor Runnels, on December 19, 1859, Bush appraised the governor of a survey of Indian lands along the 100th meridian by Jones and Brown during the previous summer. He recommended that this survey not be accepted until the correctness of the deleniations of the 100th meridian be confirmed by further astronomical observations by the Texas

17 **Ibid.**

18 **Ibid.**, pp. 266-269.

19 **Ibid.**

20 **Ibid.**

commission.[21]

In anticipation of the resumption of the work of the joint commission in the spring of 1860, Governor Sam Houston appointed William H. Russell as acting commissioner on February 1, 1860.[22] Russell accepted the appointment; he informed the governor three days later that he was ready to depart for Sherman as soon as expense money could be made available,[23] and on February 15, 1860, Russell was in Sherman making preparations for the expedition.[24]

On March 19, 1860, Secretary of War Jacob Thompson wrote Governor Houston that the United States commission would soon leave its winter quarters in Fort Smith and would be in the vicinity of Fort Arbuckle about May 10; Thompson suggested that the Texas commission join Clark at that place.[25] Because of the delay of the mail, Governor Houston did not receive the letter in time to have the commission at Fort Arbuckle on that date, but he assured the Secretary of War that the Texas commission would proceed to that point as soon as possible.[26]

In the meantime, Russell transmitted a letter to Governor Houston which he had received from Commissioner Clark, informing him that the

21 W.A. Bush to Governor Runnels, Austin, December 19, 1858, Texas State Library; J.A. Clark to Secretary of Interior Jacob Thompson, Camp in Creek Nation, October 27, 1859, **Senate Documents, Forty-seventh Congress, First Session** (Serial 2076) Doc. No. 70, Vol. III, p. 278.

22 Commission is in "State Department Boundary Papers, 1837-1911," Archives, Texas State Library.

23 William H. Russell to Governor Sam Houston, Austin, February 3, 1860, "State Department Boundary Papers, 1837-1911," Archives, Texas State Library.

24 William H. Russell to Governor Sam Houston, Sherman, February 5, 1860, **ibid.**

25 Jacob Thompson to Governor Sam Houston, Washington, March 19, 1860, **Senate Documents, Forty-seventh Congress, First Session** (Serial 2076) Doc. No. 70, Vol. III, p. 280.

26 Governor Sam Houston to Jacob Thompson, Austin, April 16, 1860, **ibid.**

United States commission expected to arrive at Fort Arbuckle on May 1, 1860; that he would proceed from that place to "Take up the 100th meridian as has already been determined at a point near the Canadian River." Russell called Governor Houston's attention to the fact that Clark contemplated the endorsement of the line along the 100th meridian from Red River northward to a point nineteen miles north of the Canadian River, which had been surveyed and marked by Jones and Brown. Russell emphasized the fact that Texas was not a party to that survey and, as Bush had advised Governor Runnels earlier, he hoped that the governor would not accept it. Russell further stated that it would be impossible for the Texas commission to be ready and at Fort Arbuckle by May 10 since he would be compelled to secure bacon from New Orleans. He thought that June 1 would be the very earliest date for travel because of scarcity of grass before that time.[27]

Governor Houston lost no time in preparation to send the commission to join Clark's party. He appointed Captain Thomas F. Chapman as secretary and B. Timmons as surveyor and ordered the Texas commission to join the United States commission at Fort Arbuckle, with instructions that if the survey were conducted upon correct basis, the only point of dispute could arise over which fork of Red River could be the prong which was specified by the treaty of limits and which was shown on the Melish Map.[28]

He continued by referring to the fact that Marcy had surveyed all three prongs to their sources; he was convinced that Marcy considered the North Fork as the Red River since he marked the spot of his encampment by burying a bottle containing "certain memoranda." Houston attached such significance to Marcy's statement on May 26, 1852, when he said that the Red River which passed through the western extremity of the Wichita Mountains was changed in character below the point of confluence with South Fork. He concluded his instructions by stating that Russell would be aided by the Melish Map; Houston urged him to insist upon the North Fork as the main Red River and as the true boundary line, but should the United States commissioner insist upon the South Fork as the Red River, Russell should cooperate but do so

27 William H. Russell to Governor Sam Houston, Sherman, April 4, 1860, State Department Boundary Papers, 183. 1911, Archives, Texas State Library.

28 Commissions in State Department Boundary Papers, 1837-1911, Archives, Texas State Library.

under written protest.[29]

In compliance with Governor Houston's order, Russell left Sherman on May 10 for Fort Cobb to join the United States commission.[30] Upon Russell's arrival, Clark informed him that he could not begin the survey at Red River; that his orders required that he begin at the point where the 100th meridian line was discontinued nineteen miles north of the Canadian River by Jones and Brown and project that line northward to its intersection with the line of 36 degrees and 30 minutes north latitude. In reporting the results of this conference to Governor Houston, Russell assured Houston that he would follow his instructions by cooperating with the United States commission under written protest, not only against starting the survey at that point but against the acceptance of that part of the line between this initial point and the Red River, since the State of Texas had no representation present when the survey was made. He assured the Governor that he would resurvey this section of the line alone.[31]

After a wait of two weeks, as the commission had no prospects of securing a military escort, the United States commission proceeded on June 1, 1860, just two days ahead of the Texas commission.[32] Upon the arrival of the commissions at the northernmost monument located nineteen miles north of the Canadian River by Jones and Brown, Russell addressed a letter to Clark, notifying him of Russell's intention of starting from that point and running the line along the 100th meridian southward to the main prong of Red River, where he would establish a marker which would be considered the southeast corner of the "Panhandle" of Texas. Although Russell invited the United States commission to participate in the survey, the arbitrary tone of the note indicated that Russell had forgotten the instructions of Governor Houston when he admonished Russell that the success of his mission

29 Governor Sam Houston to William H. Russell, Austin, April 29, 1860, Executive Record Book, Governor Sam Houston, 1859-1861, Archives, Texas State Library.

30 Report of Boundary Survey by W.I Russell, State Department Boundary Papers, 1837-1911, Archives, Texas State Library.

31 W.H. Russell to Governor Sam Houston, Camp Near Fort Cobb, 1860, **Ibid.**

32 Report on Boundary Commission by W.H. Russell, **ibid.**

depended upon cooperation with the United States commission.[33] That Russell had completely misunderstood the intentions of the Govenor that the joint commission work as a unit was shown by a letter to Houston in which he stated that the only advantage of the commissions working as a unit was protection.[34]

Upon receipt of this report, Governor Houston deplored the lack of cooperation by the Texas commission with that of the United States when he apprised Russell that special concert of action and full cooperation upon the part of the Texas commission was enjoined upon him as the head of the commission, and that such was expected of him; instead of harmony and joint action, discord and petty jealousy prevailed to the detriment of the State of Texas.[35]

In reply to the invitation by Russell to survey southward from Jones and Brown's marker nineteen miles north of the Canadian River, Clark replied that since that segment had been properly surveyed and marked, there was no reason for another survey by the United States. He therefore stated his determination to start with the northward termination of the Jones and Brown survey and proceed northward to the Arkansas River.[36] This reply showed an utter disregard of the provisions of the act of Congress by which the commission was created and under which Clark was working. The law stated specifically that the survey would start at the point of intersection of Red River with the 100th meridian and follow that meridian northward to the point where it intersects the line along 36 degrees and 30 minutes north latitude.[37] Since Russell had chosen to ignore Houston's orders to cooperate with the United States commission and because of the fact that Clark had disregarded the provisions of the act by which his commission was created, little hope for success of the project was in prospect.

As the commissions were bent on going their own way separately, the United States commission projected the line along the 100th meridian

33 Report of William H. Russell, 1816, **ibid.**

34 William H. Russell to Governor Sam Houston, Camp of Boundary Commission, July 17, 1860, **ibid.**

35 Sam Houston to William H. Russell, Austin, July 25, 1860, **ibid.**

36 Clark to Russell, Boundary Camp, June 10, 1860, Enclosed in report on Boundary Survey by W.H. Russell, 1861, **ibid.**

37 Petters (ed.), **Statutes at Large,** Vol. I, p. 310.

northward from the Jones and Brown monument situated nineteen miles north of the Canadian River to its intersection with the line along 36 degrees and 30 minutes north latitude, while the Texas commission surveyed southward from the initial point to the North Fork of Red River where it placed a monument fifteen feet in diameter and seven feet high on the north side of the river. It also placed a large wooden shaft in the center, marked on the north face, "100 west longitude," on the east, "Indian Territory," on the south, "Texas," and on the west, "Texas 1860." Having completed that portion of the line, the Texas commission returned to the point of beginning and projected the line northward, in the footsteps of the United States commission, to the line along 36 degrees and 30 minutes north latitude. Upon its arrival at the intersection of the 100th degree longitude with 36 degrees and 30 minutes north latitude, the Texas commission found that Clark had already located and marked the point of intersection. The Texas commission accepted the point as Russell did not doubt the accuracy of the calculations since the United States commission had reached its conclusions as a result of observations covering a week's time with the most modern instruments available.[38]

The joint commission thereafter retired from the field without achieving the results which both the Texas and United States officials expected. The 100th meridian line had been surveyed from the North Fork of Red River to the point of intersection of that line with the line along the parallel of 36 degrees and 30 minutes by the Texas commission. The United States commission had projected this line from the monument located nineteen miles north of the Canadian River by Jones and Brown during the previous year to the same point of intersection. Although the commissions did not work together as the laws provided, they were in agreement in regard to the location of the 100th meridian and the intersection of that meridian with 36 degrees and 30 minutes north latitude. The commissions did not agree, however, in regard to which fork of Red River was the true Red River which was shown on the Melish Map. Each government, therefore, continued its claim upon the

38 Report on Boundary Survey by William H. Russell, 1861, State Department Boundary Papers, 1837-1911, Archives, Texas State Library.

disputed area which was located between the forks of the river from north to south, and between the point of confluence of the two branches to the true 100th meridian from east to west.[39]

39 Friction developed between Clark and the commissioner of the land office before Clark's report was completed. As a result of this misunderstanding, the secretary of interior ordered the commissioner of the land office to terminate the boundary commission and transfer all papers and documents to the general land office. The documentary material, therefore, remained unfinished until 1882 when the senate ordered that the date and records be compiled. **Senate Documents, Forty-seventh Congress, First Session** (Serial 2076) Doc. No. 70, Vol. III, p. 308.

CHAPTER V

Disputed Sovereignty

Convinced that the North Fork of the Red River was the boundary line between Texas and the territory of the United States, the Texas Legislature asserted the sovereignty of Texas over the disputed area by an act passed February 8, 1860, which created Greer County, Texas, with the boundary beginning at the confluence of the North Fork and the South Fork; running up the North Fork to its intersection with the 23rd. degree of west longitude; thence south to the South Fork; thence following the channel of that stream to the point of beginning.[1]

Interest in Greer County was interrupted by the outbreak of the Civil War and, as a result, the County was not organized until after the close of the War. Following the return of peace, the authorities of Texas were particularly active in asserting and strengthening the claims of Texas to this area. It was the policy of the Texas government to attach the unorganized counties to the nearest organized county for administrative and judicial purpose; consequently, Greer County was attached to Montague County with provision that when Clay County should be organized, Greer County would be attached to it.[2] The latter part of this provision was never carried out however, since Greer County was attached to Wheeler County in July, 1879.[3] Two years later, Greer County was made a part of the newly created 35th judicial district,[4] and

1 John Sayles and Henry Sales, (eds.) **Revised Statutes of Texas,** Vol. I, p. 272.

2 H.P.N. Gamme., (ed.), **Laws of Texas,** Vol. V, p. 1012.

Ibid., Vol. IX, pp. 60-61.

4 **Ibid.,** Vol. IX, pp. 100-101.

in March of the same year, it became a part of Clay County land district.[5]

The Legislature continued its policy of strict control over Greer County by transferring this county from Clay land district to Wheeler land district in April, 1883,[6] and during the following year the county was made a part of the 35th judicial district.[7] In March, 1885, it was provided that all appeals and writs of error from Greer County would be returnable to the district court of Travis County.[8]

The state of Texas asserted sovereignty over Greer County not only by enacting these various administrative laws, but by assuming ownership of the public domain as well. On July 28, 1876, a bill was passed which provided that all indigent veterans and widows of veterans of the Texas Revolution might receive 640 acres of land from the unappropriated public lands wherever such lands might be located in the state.[9] The benefits from this act, however, were restricted by a law of February 25, 1879, which provided that all public lands embraced in the territorial limits of Greer County be set aside, one-half for public schools and the other one-half for the purpose of paying the public debt. It was further provided that the public domain be surveyed and disposed of in such manner as might be prescribed by law.[10]

The act of July 28, 1876, was not acceptable to the veterans because the benefits were too small and because it applied only to indigent recipients. Through the leadership of John M. Swisher, a veteran of the Texas Revolution, an act was passed on March 15, 1881, which provided that land certificates for 1280 acres be issued to all veterans of the Texas Revolution and veterans' widows without regard to financial status.[11] In

5 **Ibid.**, Vol. IX, p. 116.

6 **Ibid.**, Vol. IV, pp. 358-359.

7 **Ibid.**, Vol. IV, pp. 558-559.

8 **Ibid.**, Vol. IX, pp. 670-671.

9 **Ibid.**, Vol. IX, pp. 691-693.

10 **Ibid.**, Vol. VIII, p. 1316.

11 **Ibid.**, Vol. IX, 127-128; Message of O.M. Roberts to the Texas Legislature, August 10, 1883, Papers of the **Governors of Texas,** Archives, Texas State Library.

compliance with this law, the veterans and veteran's widows could locate unappropriated land, apply for a patent at the land office, and then sell the land. Since the people were eligible for this land were too old to face the hardships of frontier life, many sold their certificates for Greer County land to the Day Land and Cattle Company[12] which purchased certificates for 144,640 acres.[13] Since this land had been reserved for school purposes and for the payment of the public debt by the law of February 25, 1879,[14] the issuance of certificates on this land was provided for by the subsequent act of March 15, 1881,[15] defeated the purpose of the bill. In an attempt to correct the mistake, the Legislature passed a bill on April 1, 1881, which authorized holders and owners of patents issued on land in Greer County to surrender their patents for cancellation; the land commissioner was at the same time authorized to issue new certificates to lands elsewhere in lieu of this land.[16]

While Texas was asserting its claims to Greer County, the policy of the United States Government could have been interpreted as a surrender of claims to the disputed territory as a recognition of the Texas title to the country. On February 24, 1879, the United States Congress passed an act entitled, "An Act to Create the Northern Judicial District of the State of Texas, and to Change the eastern and western judicial districts

12 The Day Land and Cattle Company was composed of J.W. (Doc) Day, the Maddox brothers, Charlie Anderson, and John Powers. They went to Greer county in 1882 and purchased 10,000 head of cattle from Haynie and Handy at thirty six dollars for cows with calves and eighteen dollars for yearlings. **Mangum Daily Star** (Mangum, Oklahoma), October 13, 1937.

13 **Texas Reports**, 68, 528; **Mangum Daily Star**, October 13, 1937.

14 H.P.N. Gammel, ed., **Laws of Texas**, Vol. VIII, p. 1316.

15 **Ibid.**, Vol. IX, pp. 127-128.

16 **Ibid.**, Vol. IX, p. 899. When the Day Land and Cattle Company refused to surrender title to lands which they had located in Greer County with these certificates, the State of Texas sued that company for cancellation of title. The Supreme Court ruled that the titles were invald and that grant certificates could not thereafter be located in Greer County because those lands had already been set aside by the act of February 28, 1879. "Day Land and Cattle Company Versus State," **Southwestern Reporter**, Vol. IV, pp. 866-879.

of Texas, and to fix the time and place of holding courts in the districts." The first section of the act which provided for the northern judicial district included Greer County, Texas as a part of the district.[17]

In response to a petition by the people of Greer County, the post office department established post offices at Mangum and at Frazier, Greer County, Texas, on March 1, 1886.[18] When, however, it was discovered by the post office department that these newly created offices were located in the disputed territory, their designation was immediately changed from Greer County, Texas, to Greer County, Indian Territory.[19] When Postmaster Henry Sweet of Mangum was apprised of the change, he protested by a letter to Congressman Fritz Lanham of Texas on January 17, 1887. Lanham endorsed the protest and forwarded it to the post office department but nothing was done about it. Lanham did not press the case because he felt that this act would not prejudice the settlement of the qustion.[20]

In spite of the fact that Texas had assumed complete sovereignty over Greer County and that the United States had seemingly defaulted in its claim to the territory, a feeling by the inhabitants of the presence of an indefinite political jurisdiction was demonstrated in August, 1881, when James S. Irwin was tried in the district court at Mobeetie, Wheeler County, Texas, to which Greer County had been attached for judicial purposes, for a murder committed in Greer County. When the defendant was brought to trial, he entered a plea of no jurisdiction on the grounds that Greer County was not a part of Texas. Frank Willis, judge of the district court, overruled the plea by holding that Greer County was a part of Texas and that Texas state courts had jurisdiction in that county.[21]

17 Secretary of State, (ed.), **Statutes at Large,** Vol. XX, p. 318.

18 **House Reports, Fifty-eighth Congress, Second Session** (Serial 4581) Doc. No. 1595, Vol. V, p. 3; **Buckskin Joe's Immigrant Guide**, Navajoe, Greer County, Texas, March 10, 1886.

19 **Ibid.**, Vol. V, p. 2.

20 **Mangum Daily Star**, October 13, 1937.

21 Irwin was convicted of murder and was serving a life sentence in the Texas penitentiary in 1884. **House Reports, Forty-eighth Congress, First Session** (Serial 2253) Doc. No. 63, Vol. I, p. 3.

Shortly thereafter, a case came before the same court in which parties owning land in Greer County sought to escape payment of taxes to the authorities of Texas on the ground that Greer County was not a part of Texas; the court, as in the first case, upheld the sovereignty of Texas over Greer County, and the power to collect taxes.[22]

The Indian commissioner was the only official who had demonstrated any interest in maintaining jurisdiction in the disputed territory on the part of the United States Government. Under a contract dated on June 26, 1873, O.T. Merrill, United States surveyor, surveyed the public lands in townships seven to twelve inclusive, range 27 west, Indian meridian, Oklahoma. In the execution of this survey, he closed his lines on the 100th meridian as had been established by Jones and Brown.[23] In 1875, C.L. DuBois re-established the 100th meridian from Red River northward, a distance of 31 miles. DuBois developed the fact that the line of Jones and Brown had a considerable bearing to the east, averaging in the 31 miles about 2/3 of one degree. He was able to identify positively the old line on which he rebuilt with stone, the mile corners in the exact locations as had been established by Jones and Brown.[24] Also, in 1875, H.C.F. Hackenbush re-established the 100th meridian from the 67th to the 90th mile post. At every mile point he set a post properly marked, dug pits, and erected mounds of earth.[25] E.H. Darling continued the re-tracement from the 90th mile post on the north bank of the Canadian River northward to the south boundary of Kansas. He set a stone suitably marked at every mile point along this line.[26] All of these surveys were merely retracements of the Jones and Brown and the Clark surveys.

Senator Richard J. Oglesby of Illinois asked the acting commissioner of the General Land Office, L.K. Lippincott, for a report on the title to Greer County. Lippincott replied to the request by a letter dated

22 **Ibid.**, Doc. No. 63, p. 3.

23 **Senate Documents, Forty-seventh Congress, First Session** (Serial 1987) Doc. No. 70, Vol. II, p. 1.

24 **Ibid.**

25 **House Executive Documents, Fifty-ninth Congress, First Session** (Serial 4986) Doc. No. 259, Vol. 46, p. 1.

26 **Ibid.**

February 4, 1877, in which he not only gave a complete history of the boundary dispute, but set forth a summary of the claims of the United States to the territory.[27]

Upon receipt of this report, Senator Oglesby, forwarded a copy to J. Groos, Commissioner of the Texas Land Office;[28] Chief Clerk of the land office, Rhodes Fisher sent the communication to Governor R.B. Hubbard,[29] who requested that Groos supply him with a complete history of the boundary dispute. Groos explicitly stated the claims of Texas to Greer County by restating the argument that North Fork was the main channel of Red River.[30]

The disputed territory was attracting wide attention by 1887; ranchmen who had been operating in West Texas had discovered that free range had almost disappeared in that area. In order to secure permanent range where settlements were few, they went to Greer County. Haynie and Handy brought 10,000 head of cattle to the western part of the county;[31] about the same time John Powers arrived with 6,000 head; Ikard and Harrold brought 6,000 head; while the Franklin Cattle Company under the management of Colonel B.B. Groom had about 5,000 head in Greer County.[32]

Lieutenant Edwin H. Huffner of Fort Sill, chief engineer of the department of Missouri, reported to the war department on May 3, 1877, that he had a Texas Map in his possession which included the area which

27 L.R. Lippincott to Senator R.J. Oglesby, Washington, February 4, 1877, State Department Boundary Papers, 1837-1911, Archives, Texas State Library.

28 Oglesby to Groos, Washington, February 20, 1877, **ibid.**

29 Rhodes Fisher, Chief Clerk of the Land Office, to Governor R.B. Hubbard, Austin, April 16, 1877, State Department Boundary Papers, 1837-1911, Archives, Texas State Library.

30 Groos to Hubbard, Austin, April 21, 1877, **ibid.**

31 Haynie and Handy believed that Greer County was a part of Indian Territory; they settled in the western portion of the county so that if the United States government objected to their presence on Indian lands, they could easily move into Texas territory. **Mangum Daily Star,** October 13, 1937.

32 **Ibid.**, October 13, 1937.

comprised Greer County as Texas territory, while the same land in question was represented upon maps from the Indian Department as public lands. The War Department, consequently, called upon the Department of Interior for a clarification of the matter since the task of supervising the Indians in the area was assigned to the army.[33]

In response to this inquiry, J.A. Williams, land commissioner of the Department of Interior, replied that this area was a part of the public lands which had been ceded to the United States by the Chickasaw and Choctaw Indians in1866; he further stated that it was a part of the Indian Territory which had not at that time been allocated to any tribe; he continued by stating that the territory was originally defined to be within the United States by the treaty of limits with Spain on February 22, 1819; by the treaty between the United States and Mexico on January 12, 1828; by the joint resolution which provided for the annexation of Texas on March 1, 1845; by the survey of Jones and Brown, and by the surveys of Clark and Russell in 1860. Williams concluded that the land in question was within the jurisdiction of the United States and did not belong to the State of Texas as the map of the state in possession of the commanding officer at Fort Sill indicated.[34]

In December, 1881, a bill was introduced in the House of Representatives by Congressman Olin Welborn which defined the boundary between Texas and the Indian Territory as being the North Fork of Red River instead of the South Fork from the confluence of the two branches at the 100th meridian.[35] When the bill was referred to the judiciary committee of the house, Representative Edwin Willets, chairman of the committee, realized that the bill proposed to settle the dispute by legislation rather than upon the basis of legal claims. The committee reported that the land in dispute lying between the two forks of Red River and bounded on the west by 100th meridian was about sixty miles long and forty miles wide; if this valuable land was a part of Texas, the land belonged to the state under the act of its admission to the United States, while if it was a part of the Indian Territory, which branch or fork of Red River ws its main branch? The committee further observed that the initial point of investigation was the treaty between

33 **House Reports, Forty-seventh Congress, First Session** (Serial 2069) Doc. No. 1282, Vol. V, pp. 3-5.

34 **Ibid.**

35 **Ibid., Journal of the House, Forty-seventh Congress, First Session** (Serial 2008) p. 20.

the United States and Spain dated February 22, 1819, in which this part of the boundary was defined.

The committee recognized the fact that, at the time of the treaty, the region had never been accurately explored and, consequently, it was not known that Red River divided into two branches before it reached the 100th meridian. Although the committee was of the opinion that the disputed area belonged to theUnited States, it closed the report by stating that in as much as the claim was disputed with the earnestness of belief on the part of Texas, and in as much as none of the surveys had been made with the privity of Texas, that state should have a hearing in the matter and should have an opportunity to cooperate with the United States in settling the facts upon which the question in dispute rested. The committee then reported a substitute bill which provided for a joint commission for the purpose of establishing the boundary line.[36]

As nothing was done in regard to the substitute bill and since the data on the Clark survey was not available to the Senate because of the unfinished condition of his report,[37] Senator S.B. Maxey of Texas introduced a bill in the Senate in 1882 authorizing the president to appoint another commission which would work with a similar commission on the part of Texas in running and marking this boundary. Senator Maxey emphasized the earnest desire of the Texas officials to settle the qustion; he stated that the Governor of Texas had called a special session of the Legislature for the purpose of providing a commission, and that the Legislature was in session at that time for that purpose. The bill passed the Senate on April 19, 1882, but failed in the House because some of the members were convinced that ample information in regard to the boundary line had been acquired by the Jones and Brown and by the Clark surveys, consequently, the establishment of another commission would be useless duplication.[38]

In the meantime, in his message to the Legislature, Governor Elisha M. Pease reported that Senator Maxey had introduced the bill providing for the running and the establishment of the boundary line; that the

36 **House Reports, Forty-seventh Congress, First Session,** (Serial 2069) Doc. No. 1282, Vol. V, pp. 1-4.

37 **Senate Reports, Forty-seventh Congress, First Session** (Serial 2004) Doc. No. 314, Vol. I, pp. 1-2.

38 Senator Maxey to Governor Pease, Washington, May 24, 1882, Texas State Boundary Papers, 1837-1911, Archives, Texas State Library.

Department of Interior had admitted that no report of any joint commission had been made, and since the committee on territories had reported favorably on the bill, he was certain that the bill would pass. He therefore asked the legislature to provide for a commission to work with commissioners which would be provided by this bill.[39]

The Legislature responded by passing an emergency act which authorized the Governor to appoint suitable representatives, who, in conjunction with such persons as might be appointed by the United States to run and mark the boundary beginning with the point of intersection of the 32nd degree north latitude with the western branch of the Sabine River and running northward to the Red River; thence following the course of Red River to the 100th degree latitude according to the Melish Map.

The bill further provided that the commission would report its conclusions together with all necessary notes, maps, and other papers in order that the question might be definitely settled as to the true location of the 100th degree west longitude, and whether the North Fork of Red River or the South Fork were the true Red River. The commission was instructed to consider actual surveys, and measurements with such well established marks as might be found, in locating the line.[40]

Since the United States Congress had failed to provide for a commission, the question was dropped until January, 1883, when Governor John Ireland, in his message to the legislature, expressed the opinion that Texas should no longer hesitate to assert its claim to Greer County; he thought it was the duty of the state to take possession and treat it as territory to which the state had undeniable title.[41] He then informed President Chester A. Arthur that the Texas Legislature had provided for a commission to work jointly with a similar commission from the United States to establish the boundary line during the administration of his predecessor and that he could find no evidence that Governor Pease had conferred with the United States officials in regard to the subject of that law. He stated that since the United States had

39 Governor's Message to the Legislature in Special Session **Austin Statesman** (Austin, Texas), April 7, 1882.

40 **House Executive Documents, Fiftieth Congress, First Session** (Serial 2550) Doc. No. 21, Vol. VIII, pp. 6-7.

41 Message of Governor John A. Ireland to the Eighteenth Legislature, January, 1883, Miscellaneous Papers, No. 15, File Box 257, Archives, Texas State Library.

advanced claim to the territory known as Greer County, Texas, and in as much as the State of Texas felt that it had a perfect title to the territory, he urged the president to take such steps as were necessary to activate a joint commission to survey the boundary. Governor Ireland stated that a large number of people had settled in the territory and that if the respective claims of Texas and the United States were settled, the county would be rapidly settled. In order to emphasize the desire on the part of Texas to settle the question, and that the President might more thoroughly understand the object of the bill, Governor Ireland enclosed a copy of it in his communication.[42]

President Arthur referred this letter to Secretary of Interior H.M. Teller, who replied that he had been instructed by a senate resolution to furnish the Senate with a report on the survey of the United States and Texas boundary commission as was provided for under the provision of the act of Congress approved June 5, 1858. Teller was of the opinion that the 100th meridian had been correctly surveyed and that there was no use of further surveys in the field. He felt that the question to be solved was the determination as to which of the two forks of Red River was the main channel. He recommended that a joint commission be formed for the purpose of deciding this question.[43]

While this question was pending, a local rivalry between the ranchmen and the farmers of Greer County developed. The ranchmen had come to this area in search of new grass which would not soon be turned under by the plow of the farmer. By 1884, however, the ranchmen could vision a repetition of the same act of that drama which moved along the frontier from east to west across the North American continent; the act in which the ranchmen came to be crowded out by the advancing farming frontier. The ranchmen of Greer County thought that if they could persuade the United States Government to evict the farmers from the disputed territory, the country would be left to the use of the ranchmen. Colonel B.B. Groom of the Franklin Cattle Company, therefore, reported to his personal friend, Secretary of Interior H.M. Teller, that citizens were settling upon the unoccupied lands in the disputed area; he advised that the United States Government assert sovereignty over Greer County by

42 Governor John A. Ireland to President Chester A. Arthur, Austin, August 24, 1884, **Senate Documents, Forty-eighth Congress, First Session** (Serial 2166) Doc. No. 99, Vol. V, p. 1-5.

43 Secretary of Interior H.M. Teller to President Chester A. Arthur, Washington, October 1, 1884. **Ibid.**, pp. 1-4.

prohibiting this trespassing upon the public lands.[44]

Teller informed Robert Lincoln, Secretary of War, of this situation in a letter dated on June 2, 1884. He observed that this settlement was within an area claimed by Texas but had been included within the limits of the Indian Territory and had been treated as such. He further observed that in the absence of any definite settlement of the boundary line between Texas and the United States, Greer County should be treated as Indian territory. Teller therefore suggested that military force be used to evict intruders until the question could be settled.[45]

On June 25, 1884, Lieutenant C.J. Crane, stationed at Fort Sill, Indian Territory, was ordered to eject all intruders from Greer County. Should any person give a reasonable justification to the right to remain, however, Crane should report the case to headquarters before taking extreme measures. He proceeded by way of Doan's Store, Texas, with a detachment of the Seventh Cavalry to Greer County. He reported that there were not more than ten families present in the area, but there were approximately 60,000 head of cattle belonging to seven or eight firms which had employed there more than 100 men. Crane further observed that, except the portion of the county east of Salt Fork and south of Draw Springs, the land was regularly parcelled out between the cattle men, and that the Franklin Land and Cattle Company had about 40,000 head of cattle there. He reported that their small ranch and line riders were scattered from the headwaters of Red River to North Fork, and that in spite of the fact that some of the settlers and cattle firms had been there for several years, they had made no improvements whatsoever.[46]

To the surprise of the ranchmen, Lieutenant Crane served notice of ejection upon them as well as upon the farmers; some expressed their intention of complying immediately while others had to notify their employers. In only two cases did settlers advance a claim to the right to remain on the ground that they considered Greer County as a part of Texas. The agent of the Franklin Land and Cattle Company asserted

44 **Mangum Daily Star**, October 13, 1937.

45 H.M. Teller to Secretary of War Robert Lincoln, Washington, June 2, 1884, **Ibid.**, p. 34.

46 Lieutenant C.J. Crane to General C.C. Augur, Greer County Indian Territory, June 25, 1884, "The United States Complainent versus the State of Texas in Equity," **Record of the Supreme Court of the United States, october Term 1891**, No. 4 Original, Vol. I, p. 25; **Mangum Daily Star**, October 13, 1937.

that his company had been paying taxes to the State of Texas, while Henry A. Sweet contended that he occupied his own land which had been patented by the State of Texas; that he, consequently, had a right to stay. He substantiated his claim by producing a map of Texas, issued in 1882, which included Greer County.[47] He also had in his possession an official document showing what lands had been surveyed and what land had been issued by Texas land certificates. Crane did not think that force would have to be applied to remove the settlers; he did think that a date would have to be set for their departure before they would comply. He therefore asked for instructions in regard to the matter.[48] In reply to this report, General C.C. Augur fixed October 1, 1884, as the date by which the settlers must move.[49]

Henry Sweet immediately forwarded to Governor Ireland a copy of the order which Crane had given him.[50] In reply, Governor Ireland instructed Sweet to remain until he should be forcibly removed; to make a list of all property destroyed and to get the names of the people who had carried out the order.[51]

This order was more disastrous to the ranchmen than it was to the farmers; Colonel B.B. Groom, manager for the Franklin Land and Cattle Company, who had urged Secretary Teller to eject the intruders, thinking that only farmers would be ousted, made two trips to Washington in an attempt to get the order of removal rescinded.[52]

In the meantime, President Chester A. Arthur issued a proclamation

47 Sweet was one of the leading citizens of the territory; he later became postmaster at Mangum. **Mangum Daily Star**, October 13, 1937.

48 Lieutenant Crane to General Augur, Camp at Mouth of North Turkey Creek, July 5, 1884, "The United States Complainent versus the State of Texas in Equity," **Record of the Supreme Court of the United States, October Term, 1891, No. 4. Original**, Vol. I, p. 25.

49 General Augur to Lieutenant C.J. Crane, Fort Leavenworth, July 21, 1884, **Ibid.**, Vol. I, p. 26.

50 Henry M. Sweet to Governor John Ireland, Mangum, Greer County, Texas, July 6, 1884, State Department Boundary Papers, 1837-1911, Texas State Library.

51 Governor John Ireland to Henry Sweet, Austin, July 8, 1884, **ibid.**

52 **The Mangum Daily Star**, October 13, 1937.

on July 1, 1884, in which he warned those who were settling in the disputed territory that they were intruders upon Indian lands, and for the purpose of properly protecting the interests of the Indians in the territory, settlers should not be induced to migrate to the country where they would not be allowed to remain. The President admonished all persons who had settled in the territory, or those who contemplated settling there, that they would be speedily removed by military force.[53]

When Governor Ireland heard of the eviction notice and the proclamation by President Arthur, he expressed his surprise at such actions on the eve of an amicable adjustment of the boundary question. He challenged the legality of the procedure since it was based upon an act, passed in 1834, which gave the Indian agent authority to eject unlicensed traders who had violated the license law.[54] He contended that there was no law which made it unlawful for anyone else to go there even if it were an Indian reservation; that there was no complaint that the settlers had violated the law, or that they were in any way interfering with Indians. He took the position that since foreigners were not allowed to go there without license, Congress did not intend to make it unlawful for the citizens to go there without license. He concluded by requesting that the order be revoked.[55] As Teller was absent from his office when the Governor's letter arrived, Acting Secretary M.L. Joslyn did not feel disposed to act on a matter of so much importance.[56]

On September 5, 1884, Senator Richard R. Coke of Texas informed Teller that he had received a letter from L.R. Fleming of Albany, Texas, informing him that troops were notifying the people of Greer County to vacate the area by October 1, 1884. He reviewed the history of the dispute and reminded the Secretary that there was at the time a bill pending in the Senate which provided for a joint commission to settle the dispute; that the execution of the order would impose an unnecessary hardship upon the people of Greer County since their remaining there

53 **House Executive Documents, Forty-eighth Congress, Second Session** (Serial 2166) Doc. No. 99, Vol. V., p. 34.

54 Peters, (ed.), **Statutes at Large**, Vol. IV, p. 729.

55 Governor John Ireland to Secretary of Interior Henry M. Teller, Austin, July 14, 1884, State Department Boundary Papers, 1837-1911, Archives, Texas State Library.

56 M.L. Joslyn to Governor John Ireland, Washington, July 28, 1884, **ibid.**

would do no harm to either the state of Texas or to the United States. He therefore asked that the settlers be permitted to remain until the question could be settled.[57] In response to this request, Teller asked the Secretary of War that the order of removal be suspended.[58] Three days later the War Department suspended the order.[59]

On June 10, 1886, Henry Sweet presented a petition bearing the names of 163 qualified voters to the commissioners court of Wheeler County for the organization of Greer County, the court ordered an election to be held on July 10, 1886, for the purpose of organizing the county for the election of officers for the proposed county.[60] The election was duly held; those who favored the organization of the county held a substantial majority.[61] At a meeting of the Wheeler County commissioners court on July 21, 1886, the oath of office was administered to the County Judge-elect of Greer County.[62] The first session of the Greer County Commissioners Court was held on July 29, 1886, at which time the oath of office was administered to the county officials.[63]

Upon the organization of the county, the Commissioner of the Land

57 Senator Richard R. Coke to Secretary of Interior H.M. Teller Washington, September 5, 1884, "The United States Complainent **versus** the State of Texas in Equity," **Record of the Supreme Court of the United States, October Term, 1891, No. 4 Original,** Vol. 1, pp. 155-156.

58 h.m. teller to Robert Lincoln, Washington, September 23, 1884, **ibid.**, Vol. I, p. 157.

59 Robert Lincoln to H.M. Teller, September 27, 1884, **ibid.**, Vol. I, p. 157.

60 Emanuel Dabbs was county judge and Mathew Clark, W.W. Anderson, M.C. Hughes, and Henry Fry were the commissioners. Minutes of Commissioner's Court of Wheeler County, June 10, 1886, Minute Book, Vol. I, p. 40, Court House, Mobeetie, Texas.

61 Record Book of Elections of Wheeler County, Vol. I, p. 1, Court House, Mobeetie, Texas.

62 Minutes of Wheeler County Commissioner's Court, July 21, 1886, Minute Book, Vol. I, p. 41, Court House, Mobeetie, Texas.

63 Minutes of Greer County Commissioner's Court, July 29, 1886, Minute Book, Vol. I, p. 1, Court House, Mangum, Oklahoma.

Office of Texas announced his intention of surveying the land, classifying it as either school land or land to be applied to the payment of the public debt and either selling the land or leasing it. When this announcement reached the settlers of Greer County, they were exceedingly alarmed over the prospect of either being forced to purchase their homes from Texas or being ejected by another purchaser. Therefore, about 200 people attended a mass meeting at Mangum on August 29, 1886, where they discussed the matter with commissioner R.M. Hall of the Texas Land Office. They formally adopted a resolution in which they asked Hall to accept the United States surveys, recognize their homesteads, and delay the leasing of land until after January 1, 1888.

Commissioner Hall did not care to assume such grave undertakings without confirmation of his legal rights; he, therefore, asked Attorney General Stephen Hogg of Texas the question as to whether he had the right to designate, lease, and sell school lands in Greer County.[64] With the assurance that he did have the right, Hall notified the settlers that he would proceed with the classification and sale of the land.[65]

The people were thoroughly aroused over this action; this may be observed as the turning point in sentiment on the part of the small landholder away from Texas and in favor of the United States. The Texas Government had thoroughly demonstrated that the settler who had improved his land would receive neither sympathy nor consideration in the disposition of state lands. This sentiment was expressed by a letter which A.J. Meers of Vernon, Texas, wrote to A.C. Garland of Washington in which he implored Garland to use his influence with President Cleveland to put a "quietus" upon the designs of Texas to seize Greer County. He complained that people who had improved their homes, built fences, and made other improvements had not recognized claim to this land under Texas law.[66]

As a result of the numerous appeals for relief, Commissioner William Sparks of the general land office recommended to the Secretary of

64 Attorney General James Stephen Hogg to R.M. Hall, Commissioner of General Land Office, Austin, September 13, 1887, "The United States Complainent versus the State of Texas in Equity," **Record of the Supreme Court of the United States, October Term, 1894, No. 4 Original,** Vol. I, pp. 114-115.

65 **Ibid.,** p. 113; **Mangum Daily Star**, October 13, 1937.

66 A.J. Meers to Hon. A.H. Garland, Vernon, Texas, September 20, 1887, **Mangum Daily Star**, October 13, 1937.

Interior that the President be requested to issue an executive proclamation warning all persons who were claiming to act as officers of Greer County, Texas, against, either selling or disposing of any of the lands, or from attempting to exercise any authority which might be contradictory to the authority of the United States.[67]

President Cleveland, impressed by those complaints issued a proclamation on December 30, 1887, warning all persons whether they claimed to act as officers of the country or other authorities, against selling or disposing of any lands in Greer County. He further warned against the purchase of these lands; he emphasized the fact that the title might become worthless and that the purchaser would thereby lose his investment.[68]

As a result of Cleveland's proclamation, the people of Greer County passed the following resolutions at a mass meeting at Mangum on January 17, 1888; (1) No Land would be purchased from Texas; (2) Each settler would establish claim to 160 acres tracts according to the United States surveys; (3) They declared that the interests of the people would be as well protected under United States jurisdiction as they would be under Texas authority. [69]

This boundary dispute which had developed as a result of a lack of geographical knowledge of the country at the time of the signing of the treaty had by this time become more acute by the involvement of a third party, the settlers, who had acquired land and established homes in the area. Since land titles were questioned and legal jurisdiction in administration of local laws and order was in a state of chaos, it was imperative that the question be settled in order to avert bloodshed.

67 **Immigrant Guide**, October, 1887.

68 Secretary of State, (ed.), **Statutes at Large**, Vol. XXV, pp. 1483-1484.

69 **Immigrant Guide**, January 1888.

CHAPTER VI

Joint Boundary
Commission of 1886

As the dispute had reached a critical stage, the Congress became active in seeking a settlement of the problem. With this in view, an act was passed on January 31, 1885, which empowered the President to detail one or more army officers who, in conjunction with such persons as might be designated by the State of Texas, to investigate the problem by ascertaining and marking the point where the 100th meridian crossed Red River, in accordance with the terms of the treaty of 1819. It was further provided that the members of the commission should make a report of their findings to the secretary of interior who would in turn transmit the report to the next session of Congress.[1]

President Grover Cleveland appointed Major A.R. Livermore, First Lieutenant Thomas L. Casey, and First Lieutenant Lansing H. Beach as commissioners on the part of the United States. He later added Major S.N. Mansfield to the commission. He enclosed a copy of the act by which the commission was authorized as instructions to the commission.[2]

On October 9, 1885, Governor John Ireland of Texas objected to the instructions on the ground that they did not go far enough; he insisted that the pertinent point should be the location of the 100th meridian "according to the Melish Map."[3] In reply to this letter, John Edicott, Secretary of Interior, stated that the suggestion had been referred to

1 Secretary of State (ed.), **Statutes at Large**, Vol. XXIII, p. 296-297.

2 **House Executive Documents, Fiftieth Congress, First Session** (Serial 2550) Doc. No. 21, Vol. VIII, p. 5.

3 John Ireland to Secretary of Interior John Endicott, Austin, October 9, 1885, **Ibid.**, 169.

4 Secretary of Interior William Endicott to Governor John Ireland, Washington, December 8, 1885, State Department Boundary Papers, Archives, Texas State Library.

the President; that he was of the opinion that the order was sufficiently explicit to enable the commission to comply fully with the requirements of the question.[4]

Governor Ireland replied that he could not agree that this was the whole duty which developed upon the commission; he contended that the scope of the treaty between the United States and Mexico in 1836 and the subsequent acts by the United States Congress and the Texas Legislature in 1850 devolved another duty vital to a correct understanding of the treaty between the United States and Spain in 1819. He was of the opinion that both parties to the treaty knew that the Melish Map was not correct; if the signers had intended that the boundary should be along the true 100th degree, it would have been unnecessary to have added, after discussing the boundary, "All according to Melish's Map as is improved up to 1818."

Governor Ireland observed that the ascertainment of the point where the true 100th meridian crossed Red River was an easy task; but since the contracting parties were conscious of the error in Melish's Map and that it would not bear the test of demonstration, they undoubtedly intended that the boundary should be at the point where Melish located the 100th meridian on Red River. He concluded by insisting that the language of the treaty be followed in the adoption of the rules and in giving instructions to the commissioners.[5]

The correspondence in regard to the instructions to the commissioners was terminated by a letter from Indicott to Ireland on January 5, 1886, in which the Secretary of Interior stated that he had presented the matter to the President, who could see no reason why his orders on the subject did not sufficiently cover the case; he therefore declined to modify the instructions; the executive orders in the case were considered to include all that Governor Ireland suggested.[6]

In compliance with the act of the Texas Legislature of 1882, Governor Ireland appointed John T. Breckenridge, W.S. Henderson, G.R. Freeman, and W.H. Burgess as commissioners to represent Texas.[7]

5 Governor John Ireland to William Endicott, Austin, December 14, 1885, **House Executive Documents, First Session** (Serial 2550) Doc. No. 21, Vol. VIII, p. 168-169.

6 Secretary of Interior William Endicott to Governor John Ireland, Washington, January 5, 1886, **ibid.**, p. 170.

7 **Ibid.**, 6-7; Messages of Governor John Ireland to the Legislature, January 11, 1887, Messages of the Governors, Archives, Texas State Library.

When the commission met at Galveston on February 11, 1886, Colonel Mansfield, chairman of the United States commission, presented the credentials and instructions of his commission while Chairman Breckenridge of the Texas commission presented the credentials and instructions of his commission.[8] It was agreed that each commission was a unit in itself, that the two chairmen be empowered to draw up and adopt rules of procedure which would govern all meetings of the commissions. It was agreed that the two chairmen should jointly preside over the joint commission; that a member of either commission who desired to address the joint commission should be recognized by the chairmen of the commission of which he was a member and that the chairmen of the commission might adopt such additional rules as they might from time to time deem necessary.[9]

After these routine methods of procedure were agreed upon, the commission called General Randolph B. Marcy on February 26, 1886,[10] who, as a captain in the army had explored the disputed area in 1852.[11] General Marcy testified that he had never seen a copy of the Melish Map of the United States which embraced that part of the Red River country in dispute before that date. He further stated that the map showed one large fork of Red River with one more small stream to the north which was not named but might have been intended for either Washita River or Cache Creek. He was of the opinion that North Fork was the main river because its bed was much wider than that of South Fork although water covered only a small portion of its bed because of the sandy nature of the soil which readily absorbed the water. He testified that the Prairie

8 **House Executive Documents, Fiftieth Congress, First Session** (Serial 2550) Doc. No. 21, VIII, 7.

9 **Ibid.,** 6-7.

10 While Senator Maxey was in New York in December, 1885, General Marcy expressed views which would be favorable to Texas. However, since he was a retired army officer, he did not wish to volunteer information which would be detrimental to the cause of the United States; he suggested that Texas take the initiative by propounding questions in writing. Senator S.B. Maxey to Governor John Ireland, January 27, 1886, Washington, "State Department Boundary Papers, 1837-1911," Texas State Library.

11 Randolph B. Marcy, **Explorations of the Red River of Louisiana,** p. 1-12.

Dog Town Fork and the North Fork, from their confluence to their sources were about equal in length, the Prairie Dog Town Fork being 170 miles while the North Fork was 180 miles.[12]

General Marcy was of the opinion that the North Fork was the branch which was shown on the Melish Map as "Rio Roxo"; he did not think that Prairie Dog Town River was known to civilization before his explorations in 1852 because the character of the country through which the stream passed was of such a nature that travelers would not likely go that way since there was a more favorable route north of North Fork. He explained that the water in Prairie Dog Town River, from its confluence with the North Fork to within two miles of its source, was so bitter and unpalatable that his men who drank it became ill. The Indians had told him that they had avoided the river because the water was so nauseating that it sometimes proved fatal to their children. The sandy soil along the river and the formidable obstructions presented by the Staked Plains offered sufficient barrier to the Mexican traders between Santa Fe and Natchitoches that they would not have gone that way since there was a splendid route a little further north.[13]

In conclusion, General Marcy observed that Rio Roxo upon the Melish Map was entirely south and west of the Wichita Mountains which was in accord with the location of the North Fork while there were no mountains in that position from Prairie Dog Town River. He further stated that the head of the Rio Roxo upon the Melish Map was located about 37 degrees while the true latitude was about 35½ degrees. He reasoned that if Melish intended that his Rio Roxo represent the Prairie Dog Town River, the source of which was about 34½ degrees north latitude, it would be 2½ degrees too far north.[14]

Upon conclusion of this testimony, the chairman of the United States

12 **House Executive Documents, Fiftieth Congress, First Session** (Serial 2550), Doc. No. 21, VIII, p. 8-10.

13 **Ibid.**

14 The Day Land and Cattle Company sent a representative to New York to interview General Marcy in behalf of Texas; that company paid Marcy's expenses from New York to Galveston in order that he might testify. This company owned 144,640 acres of land which it wanted to protect. "The United States Complainent versus the State of Texas in Equity," **Record of the Supreme Court of the United States, October Term, 1891, No. 4 Original,** Vol. I, 334-335; **House Executive Documents, Fiftieth Congress, First Session** (Serial 2550) Doc. No. 21, p. 8-10.

commission reviewed the history of the joint commission which concluded its work in 1860,[15] as well as the work of Jones and Brown who surveyed the 100th Meridian.[16] In support of the contention of the United States commission that the Prairie Dog Town River was the main branch of Red River, Colonel Mansfield cited the statement of Jones and Brown that this branch was more than three times as wide from high water mark to high water mark than the North Fork.[17] He further stated that the act by the Texas Legislature which authorized the commission had in view that exact location of the meridian and the determination as to whether the North Fork or the Prairie Dog Town Fork was the true Red River as was designated in the treaty of 1819 with Spain. Chairman Mansfield assured the Texas commission that the United States commission was ready to cooperate in the astronomical and hydraulic determinations and would recommend that the examination be extended over a period of a year or more if no other criterion could be found which would enable them to determine the true Red River.[18]

He was cognizant of the fact that the Texas commission was authorized to use maps and other data by the act which provided for the commission; he pledged the cooperation of his commission in making available all records and knowledge at its command. Mansfield agreed to first examine the Melish Map; he stated that he was aware that the treaty map did not correspond with the true deleniations of the country in regard to the location of the larger streams and mountains. He observed that the treaty only took cognizance of what Melish indicated on the map and not what he intended to represent; he was aware that the intentions were hypothetical and not sufficiently clear as to settle the boundary question to the satisfaction of both parties.[19]

The United States commission wished to disclaim any opinion based

15 **Senate Documents, Forty-seventh Congress, First Session** (Serial 1987) Doc. No. 70, Vol. II, p. 282.

16 **House Documents, Fifty-ninth Congress, First Session** (Serial 4986) Doc. No. 259, Vol. 46, pp. 4-5.

17 **Ibid.**

18 **House Executive Documents, Fiftieth Congress, First Session** (Serial 2550), Doc. No. 21, Vol. VIII, p. 11-16.

19 **Ibid.**

solely upon the theory that Melish thought that the streams descending from the neighborhood of Taos represented any of the particular forks of Red River; Colonel Mansfield believed that the Prairie Dog Town Fork corresponded most nearly with the Red River which was delineated on the map though he did not claim that Melish was aware of it. He thought that the task of the entire joint commission was to determine whether the Prairie Dog Town Fork or the North Fork was the true Red River which was designated in the treaty between Spain and the United States in 1819. Mansfield felt that the first duty was to test the accuracy of reports at hand; if they proved to be erroneous, Mansfield thought that the joint commission should decide which of the two streams was the wider, which was the longer, which drained the larger area, which showed the greater flow of water, and which corresponded most nearly with the boundary as was laid down on the Melish Map.[20]

The United States Commission believed that the Prairie Dog Town Fork came more nearly fulfilling these requirements because it corresponded in position with Red River as was laid down by Melish; it compared more nearly in direction with the course of Red River; it was longer than the North Fork; it was wider and deeper at its intersection with the 100th meridian; it drained a larger area; and it appeared to contribute more water to the main stream throughout the year.[21] Mansfield concluded his argument by professing sincerity in his conclusions, but he emphasized the fact that he was not dogmatic in his convictions; he reminded the commission that he was open to conviction on all points.[22]

The chairman of the Texas commission made a report on March 8, 1886, in which he, for the purpose of narrowing the controversy to the fewest possible propositions consistent with the duties imposed, submitted a statement of the acts by which the joint commission was created, facts which required no proof, and claims of Texas which would be supported by evidence. Breckenridge then traced the boundary line according to the treaty of 1819, emphasizing the fact that the point where the 100th meridian crossed Red River, as was described in the treaty, had never been established by any authority. He was of the opinion that the joint commission was handicapped in its work by the variance in the objectives which were expressed by the acts which provided for the joint

20 **Ibid.**

21 **Ibid.**

22 **Ibid.**, 15.

commission.The act by the Legislature of Texas stated that the commission "Shall run and mark the boundary line between the territories of the United States and the State of Texas as laid down in the Melish Map,"[23] whereas the act of the United States Congress provided that the commission "Shall ascertain and mark the point where the 100th meridian crosses the Red River in accordance with the terms of the treaty of 1819.[24]

Breckenridge continued by assuming that the State of Texas by virtue of the treaties between the United States and the Republic of Mexico,[25] and between the United States and the Republic of Texas,[26] was subrogated and entitled to every right, privilege, and title concerning the boundary in dispute to which the Kingdom of Spain was entitled under the treaty of 1819.[27] The chairman further assumed that the joint commission must ascertain and mark the point where the 100th meridian crossed Red River in accordance with the terms of the treaty; if it should find that this meridian should be west of the line which Melish indicated on his map, and west of the confluence of the North Fork and the Prairie Dog Town Fork, it would not only be the duty of the joint commission to ascertain which of the two streams was Red River according to the terms of the treaty, but, in case of disagreement as to which was Red River, to establish the 100th meridian on both streams.[28]

Breckenridge refuted the claim of the United States commission that the 100th meridian was located west of the confluence of the North Fork and the Prairie Dog Town rivers on the ground that the line was not only surveyed without the knowledge and presence of the Texas officials, but on the ground that it did not correspond to the Melish line in regard to its position in relation to well known permanent objects such as the great bend in the Arkansas River, the mouth of the Canadian River, the range of the Wichita Mountains, the bend of the Red River northward as shown

23 **Ibid.**, 6-7.

24 **Ibid.**, 18.

25 Malloy (ed.), **Treaties and Conventions**, Vol. I, p. 1099.

26 **Ibid.**, Vol. II, p. 1779.

27 **American State Papers, Foreign Relations**, Vol. V, p. 127.

28 **House Executive Documents, Fiftieth Congress, First Session** (Serial 2550), Doc. No. 21, Vol. VIII, p. 18.

on Melish's Map, and the watershed and great basin toward the source of the Red River.[29]

Chairman Breckenridge concluded by asserting that the Rio Roxo as described in the treaty of 1819 was that which was called "North Fork" for the first time in 1852; that this stream was known to civilized man in 1819 and was delineated on Melish's Map and that the boundary line was intended to follow the course of that stream. If, however, in ascertaining the 100th meridian, the meridian should be found to cross both the North Fork and the South Fork, he contended that the North Fork should be declared as Red River.[30] In submitting the claims and issues in the case, he assured the joint commission that the Texas commissioners had done so with the evidence before it; he admitted that it might have committed some errors which would require correction upon examination of evidence which might be later introduced.[31]

On March 11, 1886, the chairman of the United States Commission agreed that the State of Texas was entitled to all the privileges which Spain enjoyed under the treaty of 1819 except insofar as the state, by its own act or acquiescence, might have committed itself to a definite and specific interpretation of the treaty. Mansfield not only accepted the assumption by the Texas commission in regard to authorized powers of the joint commission, but he contended that it was the duty of the joint commission to ascertain whether the North Fork or the Prairie Dog Town River was the true Red River of the treaty. He contended, however, that the joint commission was not authorized to define and mark the point of intersection before it had ascertained which was the main Red River. He therefore suggested that the joint commission undertake the field work which would be necessary in the solution of the problem.[32]

In speaking for the Texas commission on March 11, 1886, Breckenridge refused to recognize the assumption that the 100th meridian crossed the Prairie Dog Town River, not because it might not be found to be true, but because Texas had never been a party to any survey of the line. If, however, scientific observations by both parties should establish the meridian on the Prairie Dog Town Fork, he would agree to the truth

29 **Ibid.**, 16-18.

30 **Ibid.**

31 **Ibid.**

32 **Ibid.**, 20-21.

71

but not to the line as the boundary which was delineated on the Melish Map. For the same reason, he denied the assumption of the United States Commission that Prairie Dog Town Fork was wider, longer, carried more water, and drained a larger area. Even should that be established in the field, Breckenridge contended that this fact would not prove that the Prairie Dog Town River was the Rio Roxo of the treaty of 1819. He was willing to examine the territory, to make surveys, and collect data in regard to the matter; whatever might be the results, he would not settle the question on the basis of these findings.[33]

After an adjournment in order to give the Texas Commission time to collect evidence,[34] the Joint Commission reassembled in Austin on June 5, 1886. On the following day, Colonel Mansfield, Chairman of the United States Commission, presented evidence in support of the previous claims of the United States Commission. That the Prairie Dog Town Branch was known before 1819, was supported by extracts from Bean's account of Nolan's expedition in 1800 in which allusion is made to an Indian camp which was supposed to be located on that river, reference was made to Humboldt, Pike, and others; that the Prairie Dog Town River was the main Red River was supported by references from Captain Marcy's expedition in 1852, and that the Prairie Dog Town River was the Rio Roxo of the Melish Map was supported by a comparison of late maps with the Melish Map.[35] On June 5, 1886, the Texas Commission presented deputations of John S. Ford, Hugh F. Young, G.C. Erath, and others in substantiation of the Texas claim that the North Fork was the larger and had always been considered the main branch of Red River.[36]

As both commissions had thoroughly discussed their views and offered supporting evidence, each commission now presented resolutions to be voted on by the joint commission. In order that the joint commission might express its opinion upon the various issues which had been presented, Colonel Mansfield, in behalf of the United States Commission, offered a resolution which stated that the South Fork of Red River was wider, longer, drained a larger area, and that it corresponded more

33 **Ibid.**

34 **Ibid.**, 21.

35 **Ibid.**, 23.

36 **Ibid.**, 22-28.

37 **Ibid.**, 165-166.

nearly to the Red River than did the North Fork, as was indicated on the treaty map. He further suggested that the South Fork be designated as the boundary line and that a monument be placed at the point of intersection of the 100th meridian with that stream.[37]

Breckenridge then submitted a resolution which stated that since the North Fork ran through red clay while the South Fork ran through white gypsum, it was more logical to conclude that the North Fork was the true Red River. He further supported this claim by the fact that the North Fork was a bolder stream and that it discharged as much water as did the South Fork. He reminded the joint commission that the South Fork was known as Prairie Dog Town River and had never been designated as "Red River" until after General Marcy's discovery in 1852. Breckenridge observed that the Spanish road which was shown on the north side of Red River by the Humboldt and Melish maps was discernible along the north bank of the North Fork. He therefore asked the commission to declare the North Fork of Red River as the true Red River and the boundary line between Texas and the United States territory.[38]

The joint commission agreed that it should mark the point where the 100th meridian crossed Red River; that if this meridian should be found to be west of the confluence of the two forks, the boundary should follow the stream which best satisfied the provisions of the treaty of 1819; that the Prairie Dog Town River was longer, wider, and drained a larger area than did the North Fork; that the Red River east of the 100th meridian had never been surveyed, yet it had been indisputably considered the boundary line since 1819; that the North Fork ran through red clay formations which discolored the water while the Prairie Dog Town River ran through white gypsum formations; that that the South Fork had been known exclusively as Prairie Dog Town River before 1852. None of the fundamental points in the arguments of the commissioners was agreed upon; the reservations in those which were partially agreed upon were of such a nature that the agreements were rendered useless.[39]

On July 16, 1886, the joint commission passed a resolution declaring that everything had been accomplished that was possible under the circumstances, and that adjournment was in order until further instructions might be received. The United States Commission

38 **Ibid.**, 166-167.

39 **Ibid.**, 168.

submitted its final report to the Secretary of Interior on December 15, 1886;[40] the Texas Commission made a detailed report to Governor John Ireland of Texas.[41]

40 **Ibid.**

41 A complete journal of the proceedings of both the Texas commission and the joint commission was attached to the report by the Texas commision to Governor Ireland of Texas. "State Department Boundary Papers, 1837-1911," Archives, Texas State Library.

CHAPTER VII

The Greer County Case

The act of Congress of May 2, 1890, which provided for the temporary government of the Territory of Oklahoma also recognized the controversy in regard to the disputed boundary line along the 100th meridian. This act did not apply to that area along the 100th meridian until the boundary between the Red River and the north boundary line along 36 degrees and 30 minutes north latitude might be established. In order that a speedy designation of this line might be effected, the attorney general of the United States was authorized to file a suit in equity in the supreme court of the United States, as a court of original jurisdiction, against the state of Texas in behalf of the United States, setting forth the claim of the United States to Greer County, so that a rightful title to that area might be determined.[1]

In a letter dated May 29, 1890, Attorney General W.H. Miller informed the speaker of the house, Thomas B. Reed, that the act which created Oklahoma Territory provided that the Attorney General of the United States prosecute a law suit in behalf of the United States against the State of Texas for the purpose of settling the title to Greer County. Miller asked for an appropriation to defray expense for additional counsel and other incidentals pertaining to the suit.[2] In response to this request, the Congress appropriated 13,000 dollars on September 30, 1890.[3]

The Attorney General filed the original suit in equity in the Supreme Court on October 27, 1890. In setting forth the arguments in the case, the

1 Secretary of State, (ed.), **Statutes at Large**, Vol. XXVI, p. 92.

2 Attorney General W.H. Miller to Thomas B. Reed, Speaker of the House, Washington, May 28, 1890, **House Executive Documents, Fifty-first Congress, First Session** (Serial 2752), Doc. No. 404, Vol. XXXVII, p. 1.

3 Secretary of State, (ed.), **Statutes at Large**, Vol. XXVI, p. 528.

plaintiff laid down the following principles and claims on which the decision should be based: (1) That the intention of the two governments, Spain and the United States, as gathered from the words of the treaty of 1819, must control and that the map to which the contracting parties referred was to be given the same effect as it had been expressly made a part of the treaty; (2) Although they took the Melish Map Improved to 1818 as a basis for the final settlement of the question of boundary, they contemplated that the line was to be subsequently established with more precision by commissioners and surveyors representing the respective countries; (3) That the reference to the 100th meridian was the meridian which would be astronomically located and not necessarily the meridian located on the Melish Map; (4) That the Melish Map located the 100th meridian far east of the true meridian; (5) That the Compromise Act of 1850 provided that the boundary should be established, 'Following the course of Rio Roxo westward to the degree of longitude 100 west from London' must be interpreted as the true 100th degree and not the 100th degree according to the Melish Map; (6) That the Prairie Dog Town Fork of Red River is the continuation of Red River of the treaty; (7) That the Act of Congress which created the Northern Judicial District of Texas was to be construed as placing Greer County in that district for judicial purposes only, and not ceding the territory to Texas.[4]

Miller then reviewed the controversy from the signing of the Treaty of 1819[5] through the treaty with Mexico in 1836,[6] the treaty with the Republic of Texas in 1838,[7] and the joint resolution of 1845 by which Texas became a state of the Union.[8] He stressed the provision in Article One of the convention between the Republic of Texas and the United States which provided that each party would appoint a commissioner and a surveyor who would meet within one year from the ratification of the convention for the purpose of running and marking the boundary line from the mouth of the Sabine River to the Red River. He further

4 "The United States Complainent versus the State of Texas in Equity," **United States Reports**, Vol. CLXII, pp. 1-2.

5 **American State Papers, Foreign Relations**, Vol. IV, pp. 623-625.

6 Malloy, (ed.), **Treaties and Conventions**, Vol. I, p. 1099.

7 **House Documents, Twenty-fifth Congress, Third Session** (Serial 344), Doc. No. 2, Vol. II, p. 34.

8 Peters, (ed.), **Statutes at Large**, Vol. V, pp. 797-798.

reviewed the provision of Article Two, by which it was agreed that the remaining portion of the boundary should be run and marked at the convenience of both parties; that until this should be done, each party should exercise, without interference of the other, jurisdiction to the same extent as had been exercised before the convention.[9]

The Attorney General stated that no further action was ever taken to mark the boundary line under the treaty; that the line was still undecided when Texas was admitted to the Union in 1845. In reciting the conditions of this agreement, he stated that Texas was admitted into the Union with "The territory properly included within and rightfully belonging to the Republic of Texas." The Attorney General concluded that, by this admission, a boundary line which had been an international line became a boundary line between the United States and the State of Texas.[10]

The Attorney General claimed that a period of forty years had elapsed without action in regard to the establishment of the true boundary; he categorically accepted the line which was located by Jones, Brown, and Clark as the true 100th meridian, although he admitted that these surveys were not made jointly with Texas as the treaty provided. He complained that Texas had incorporated the territory into Greer County, Texas;[11] that Texas had exercised jurisdiction over the area in dispute until the creation of the second joint boundary commission in 1885;[12] and that the State of Texas, without title, had seized the area and extended its jurisdiction without regard to the claim of the United States. Miller further charged in the bill that in 1887 Texas had given public notice that the lands would be surveyed and placed upon the market for sale; that those who did not possess title by the authority of Texas would be

9 **House Documents, Twenty-fifth Congress, Third Session** (Serial 344), Doc. No. 2, Vol. II, p. 34.

10 "The United States Complainent versus the State of Texas in Equity," **Record of the Supreme Court of the United States, October Term, 1894, No. 4, Original,** Vol. I, pp. 1-11.

11 John and Henry Sayles, (eds.), **Revised Statutes of Texas,** Vol. I, p. 272.

12 Secretary of State, (ed.), **Statutes at Large,** Vol. XXIII, pp. 296-297.

ejected from their lands.[13]

The Attorney General reviewed the action of the President in his issuance of a proclamation in 1887, warning all the prospective land owners of the risks involved in the acquisition of Texas titles until the boundary line could be established.[14] In conclusion, he stated that since the United States could get relief in a court of equity where all the factors involved could be presented, he was filing this original bill in which Texas was made the defendant.[15]

Augustus H. Garland, John Hancock, George Clark, and H.J. May as counsel for the State of Texas filed the original answer to this bill in which they demurred; they contended that the determination of a boundary line was political in nature and was not susceptible to judicial determination by the Supreme Court in the exercise of its jurisdiction as was provided in the constitution. They contended that the question was not only political in nature, but that it was contrary to the rules which govern controversies between states of the Union. Counsel for the State of Texas cited authorities to support its contention that a controversy respecting the boundary of two independent nations was generally recognized as a political and not as a judicial question; that in the discussion of such a question, the courts in every country must respect the will of the legislative power in that it was the legislative branch and not the judicial which ratified treaties with foreign nations.

Counsel for Texas pointed out that this rule applied to the treaty between the United States and Spain in 1819;[16] between the United States and the Republic of Mexico in 1836;[17] and between the United

13 "The United States Complainent versus the State of Texas in Equity," **Record of the Supreme Court of the United States, October Term, 1894, Nov. 4 Original**, Vol. I, pp. 1-11.

14 **House Executive Documents, Forty-eighth Congress, Second Session** (Serial 2166), Doc. No. 99, Vol. V, p. 34.

15 "The United States Complainent versus the State of Texas in Equity," **Record of the Supreme Court of the United States, October Term, 1894, No. 4 Original**, Vol. I, pp. 1-11.

16 **American State Papers, Foreign Relations**, Vol. IV, pp. 623-625.

17 Malloy, (ed.), **Treaties and Conventions**, Vol. I, p. 1099.

States and the Republic of Texas in 1838.[18] It could not see why, after the admission of Texas into the Union, a different principle should apply; counsel for Texas contended that these treaties were intact and were the contracts which defined and regulated the relations of the contracting parties; that the method which was provided for in these treaties for the settlement of differences which might arise, was the only method by which this quesiton could be settled; and that these treaties specifically stipulated that the boundary line should be determined by commissioners appointed by the respective powers. It concluded, therefore, that in its inception, the question was political and not judicial in nature and consequently, the Court did not have jurisdiction.[19]

Even though the Court should be of the opinion that the controversy should be a judicial question and analogous to boundary differences between states of the Union, of which the Court had original jurisdiction, counsel for the State of Texas further demurred on the ground that the judicial powers of the United States, and especially the original jurisdiction of the Supreme Court, did not extend to controversies between the United States and individual states.[20]

Counsel for Texas recognized the original jurisdiction of the Court in cases where the United States is a party to controversies between states, between state and a citizen of another state, and between a state or a citizen thereof and a foreign nation. It further conceded jurisdiction in cases affecting ambassadors, other public ministers and counsels, and those in which a state should be a party. It observed, however, that whenever a state was mentioned in the clause declaring the extent of judicial powers, the opposite party to the controversy was also mentioned; that in no case did it include the United States. Texas counsel insisted that the parties with whom a state could have a legal controversy were distinctly named and that all others were necessarily excluded; that in no instance could the Court function in a controversy between a state and the United States.[21]

18 **House Documents, Twenty-fifth Congress, Third Session** (Serial 344) Doc. No. 2, Vol. II, p. 34.

19 "The United States Complainent versus the State of Texas in Equity," **United States Reports**, Vol. CXLIII, p. 625.

20 **Ibid.**, pp. 625-626.

21 Garland, Hancock, Clark, and May based this argument on **The Constitution of the United States**, Article III, Section 2.

The Texas counsel further demurred on the ground that the boundary line of the treaty of 1819 was designated as the "Whole being as laid down in Melish's Map of the United States, Published at Philadelphia, Improved to the First of January, 1818." It contended that the Melish Map became an essential part of the description of the boundary; without it, neither the Court nor the defendant was informed clearly as to the limits of the claims of the United States, nor to the extent of the territory claimed by the complainant in the bill since the map was a component part of the treaty and since the complainant had not attached a copy to the bill; the counsel for the State of Texas contended that the bill was defective and, consequently, should not be considered by the Court.[22]

The counsel for Texas then filed a motion in which it presented an additional point of demurrer on the ground that the complainant's case of action was legal and not equitable, and that it was a suit of action to recover certain real property which was described by the defendant in the bill; that if the complainent had a right to recover, it must be done in a court of law and not in a court of equity. It contended that since this was true, the act of Congress which authorized the suit was unconstitutional; it therefore asked the Court to dismiss the case.[23]

In consideration of the points of this demurrer, the Court recognized the necessity of the suit in equity as a measure of peace between the Government of the United States and the State of Texas. It stated that the nature and importance of the question raised by the demurrer would appear from a statement of the principal facts which were disclosed by the bill. The Court reviewed the treaties between the United States and Spain in 1819; between the United States and Mexico in 1836; and between the United States and Texas in 1838, all of which provided that the boundary line would be established by a joint commission. The treaty of annexation in 1845 stipulated that "The territory properly included within and rightfully belonging to the Republic of Texas may be erected into a state," with certain conditions. The Court traced the provisions of the Compromise of 1850 in which it was agreed that a portion of the Texas boundary should follow the 100th meridian from Red River to its intersection with a line along 36 degrees and 30 minutes north latitude; that Texas would cede to the United all its claims exterior to these limits

22 "The United States Complainent versus the State of Texas in Equity," **Record of the Supreme Court of the United States, October Term, 1894, No. 4 Original**, Vol. I, pp. 11-12.

23 **Ibid.**, p. 42.

for a consideration of $10,000,000 dollars. [24]

The Court stated that during a period of about forty years after 1819, no other action was taken in an attempt to settle the boundary question. In consideration of the contention of Texas that the ascertainment of the boundary was political in nature and not susceptible to judicial determination, the Court ruled that the authority which the State of Texas had offered in support of this contention applied to disputes between independent nations and had no application to a question of that nature which might exist between the Government of the United States and one of the States of the Union. It refuted the argument by citing Article Nine of the Articles of Confederation in which it was provided that the last resort on an appeal in a dispute between two states was a special tribunal created by Congress. [25]

The Court stated that at the time of the adoption of the Constitution, there existed controversies between eleven states in regard to boundaries; that the necessity for the creation of some procedure for the settlement of controversies under the new government had been conceived by the Framers; and that the power was delegated to the Supreme Court which had exercised such power in many instances. It therefore denied the theory that a question of boundary between a territory of the United States and one of the states of the Union was of political nature and was not susceptible to judicial review. [26]

The important question was whether the Court could, under the Constitution, take cognizance of an original suit brought by the United States against a state to determine the boundary between one of the territories and a state. The Court observed that if it did not have original jurisdiction, the controversy must be settled by mutual agreement, by the initiation of a suit in a State Court with the consent of the State, or by war. The Court was of the opinion that if the United States did not have authority to sue in the United States Courts and should be compelled to sue in State Courts, the enforcement of all rights, powers, contracts, and privileges in their sovereign capacity would be at the mercy of the States, a condition which would be adverse to both the letter and the spirit of the constitution. The Court concluded that if it

24 George Minot, (ed.), **United States Statutes at Large**, Vol. IX, p. 446.

25 **Ibid.**, Vol. III; "The United States Complainent versus the State of Texas in Equity," **United States Reports**, Vol. CLXII, pp. 630-648.

26 **Ibid.**

had original jurisdiction in "All cases affecting ambassadors or other public ministers and consuls, and those in which a State shall be a party," it had original jurisdiction in all cases of law and equity in which a State was a party.

The Court said that the question as to the suability of Texas by the United States rested upon the right of a Government, established upon the common benefits of the people of all the States, to submit to judicial solution of controversies arising between the United States Government and any State of the Union, each sovereign with respect to the objects committed to it but both subject to the supreme law of the land. Therefore, since the Constitution was the supreme law of the land and since the Constitution gives to the Supreme Court original jurisdiction over disputes in which a State of the Union or a Territory of the United States is a party, the Court held that it had jurisdiction in this case.

In regard to the contention of Texas that a court in equity had no authority to decide the case, the Court ruled that this was not a suit simply to determine the legal title to land; that it involved the larger question of governmental authority and jurisdiction over territory. The Court ruled that the United States was asking for the execution of the terms of the Treaty of 1819 to the end that disorder and public chaos might be prevented. It concluded that the agreement embodied in the treaty to fix the boundary and establish landmarks could not be enforced by an action at law.27

Chief Justice Melville W. Fuller and Justice L.Q.C. Lamar dissented on the ground that the Court had original jurisdiction in two classes of cases only: those affecting ambassadors, other public ministers and consuls; and those in which a state should be a party. They contended that the judicial powers extended to controversies between two or more states, between a state and a citizen of another state, and between a state or a citizen thereof and foreign states, citizens or subjects of foreign nations. They said that judicial power extended to controversies to which the United States might be a party but such controversies were not included in that case.28

The defendant admitted all the facts in the bill except the allegation that a period of forty years elapsed after the conclusion of the treaty in 1819 without any action in regard to the establishment of the line though the dispute had existed during the entire time. It asserted that no

27 "The United States Complainent versus the State of Texas in Equity," **United States Reports**, Vol. CXLIII, pp. 143, 630-648.

28 **Ibid.**, pp. 648-649.

controversy had existed until a short time preceding the filing of the suit and that the "Pretended claim of complainant to the territory now in controversy was first assumed and asserted nearly forty years after the treaty was made." It further stated that this assumption had been made by subordinate military and civil officers upon conditions of "pretended geographical facts," which did not exist until thirty years after the date of the treaty.

The defendant contended that the Spanish Government was well informed in regard to the geography of the Red River country and that the Spanish officials had familiarized the Americans in regard to this matter; that the Spanish for 100 years had owned the country; that extensive military and colonial establishments had been maintained throughout the region and that a system of roads transversed it in many directions. It said that the Rio Roxo of Natchitoches had long been familiar to Spaniards and that the road from Santa Fe to Natchitoches passed through the disputed region along the banks of the North Fork long before 1819. The defendant asserted that no claims had ever been asserted to the region before Captain Marcy's exploration in 1852 at which time the South Fork was discovered; and without authority, its name was changed to "South Fork" or "Main Red River."

The defendant further avowed that the South Fork and the North Fork were so totally dissimilar that the South Fork never had been designed as "Rio Roxo." It argued that the north branch was the true Red River of the Treaty of 1819; that it was a large, fixed, and permanent stream which flowed through red clay formations to such an extent that the water was red in color.

The defendant then turned to the question of the line along the 100th meridian; it denied that this line should be established along the true 100th meridian but contended that it should be along that meridian "According to the Melish Map." In reference to the compromise bill of 1850 which stipulated that the boundary should be located on the true 100th meridian, it waived all claim to lands east of that line and between the North Fork and the line of 36 degrees and 30 minutes north latitude, but contended that the compromise did not apply to that part which extended from the North Fork to the South Fork, as the United States claimed. The defendant reasoned that the agreement in the Treaty of 1819 rested upon the same basis as that of an agreement between two individuals, and that an estoppal existed upon each government, forbidding either to claim anything upon the other in contravention to the terms of the contract.

The attorneys for Texas cited the reimbursement by the United States to Texas for the arms and equipment which were seized by

United States military forces from Major Sively in the disputed area as an acknowledgement of Texas sovereignty there.[29] They contended that the establishment of a United States post office at Mangum, Greer County, Texas, was further evidence that the United States Government had no intention of establishing claim to Greer County at that time. They emphasized the fact that Texas had continuously exercised jurisdiction over the disputed area; that Texas had created Greer County in 1860; that county government had been organized in 1886; that schools had been established; that courts had been organized; that the area had been included in legislative and senatorial districts; and that public lands had been surveyed and sold under Texas Title. The defendants denied the legality of the Jones, Brown, and Clark surveys; they contended that neither the question of boundary nor the findings of that commission should prejudice the cause of the State of Texas in the controversy. They were of the opinion that this commission was only empowered to report its findings.

In further answer to the complainant, the attorneys for the State of Texas asserted that by a true and proper construction of the terms of the treaty of 1819, the United States had never been the rightful owner of the territory in controversy, nor was it contemplated by the makers of the treaty that any necessity then existed, or would ever exist, for surveying the boundary along Red River. They were of the opinion that the contracting parties conceded that the river was a well known and established stream; that the only lines that would ever be run were that part between the Sabine River and the Red River and that which ran northward from Red River according to the Melish Map.[30]

The attorneys for the United States filed an amended bill in which they not only repeated the points in the original bill but cited the provisions of the Compromise of 1850 in which the boundary line was mutually agreed upon, whereby the line would run along the true 100th meridian of west longitude from the point of intersection of that meridian with the Red River, northward to the point of its intersection with the line along 36 degrees and 30 minutes north latitude; and that all lands east of that line were relinquished by Texas to the United States. They therefore took the position that this agreement superseded the

29 George Minot, (ed.), **United States Statutes at Large**, Vol. IX, p. 168.

30 "The United States Complainent versus the State of Texas in Equity," **Record, Supreme Court of the United States, October Term, 1891, No. 4, Original**, Vol. I, pp. 12-25.

terms of the treaty of 1819; that the United States was entitled to the territory east of that line even though the line according to the Melish Map was located far to the east.[31]

The attorneys for Texas then filed an amended bill in which they asserted that there was no point presented in the amended bill of the complainant which was not answered in their original reply; they only reaffirmed the arguments of their original reply.[32]

The attorneys for the United States replied by filing an amended answer in which they reserved all advantages of exceptions to the insufficiency of the answer by the State of Texas, and gave notice that they would file necessary evidence to support their contentions.[33]

Both the complainant and the defendant, consequently, offered a voluminous amount of documentary evidence covering the entire history of the question from the signing of the treaty of 1819 to 1890 with copies of available maps of the disputed territory as well as depositions of witnesses to support the respective arguments.[34]

The Court reviewed the evidence which had been submitted, much of which it considered worthless. It was of the opinion that the paramount question to be decided was whether South Fork or North Fork was the Rio Roxo which was delineated on the Melish Map. It refuted the Texas claim that the United States admitted that Snively was on Texas soil when the United States reimbursed Texas for seizure of arms and equipment by stating that the point of dispute was the conduct of Captain St. George Cook and not for invasion of Texas territory.

It ruled that the inclusion of Greer County in the Northern Judicial District of Texas could not be construed to imply that Congress intended to recognize Greer County as a part of Texas since judicial districts did not adhere to state lines.

The fact that the post office was first designated as Greer County, Texas, did not indicate to the court that the United States had conceded Texas jurisdiction because the Post Office Department changed the designation as soon as postal officials learned that the post office was situated in the disputed area. The Court further assumed that the Texas argument, that the State had organized Greer County and had exercised

31 **Ibid.**

32 **Ibid.**, Vol. I, p. 41.

33 **Ibid.**, Vol. I, pp. 43-44.

34 **Ibid.**, Vol. II, pp. 713-1392; Vol. I, pp. 44-712.

jurisdiction over it, did not establish title because the United States had constantly disputed that claim.

The Court then found that Greer County constituted no part of the territory properly included either within or rightfully belonging to Texas at the time of admission of the State into the Union; that it was at that time neither within the limits nor under the jurisdiction of that State, but was under the exclusive jurisdiction of the Government of the United States.[35]

On January 15, 1901, a congressional act was approved which provided for the location of the true 100th meridian by the most accurate and scientific methods.[36] In pursuance of this act, Arthur H. Kidder, Examiner of Surveys, established the point of intersection of the 100th meridian with Red River in 1902. He found the point to be 3,699.7 feet east of the Jones and Brown monument.[37] Kidder placed a stone monument 45 inches on the meridian at a point 1,563 feet north of Red River.[38] Upon instructions dated March 12, 1903, Kidder retraced the 100th meridian from the Red River to Darling's 44th cornerstone, a distance of 134 miles from Red River, or to a point a little over 1.25 miles north of parallel 36 degrees and 30 minutes.[39] He found that in the first 31 miles north of Red River the Jones-Brown line veered so far to the east as to decrease the distance from the true meridian to about 1,892.9 feet, or about half the error at the initial monument; near the Canadian River, the distance was found to be 1,234 feet. The nearest point of approach of the two lines was found at a distance of 124 miles from Red River where the old line was only 564 feet west of the true meridian.[40]

35 "The United States Complainent versus the State of Texas in Equity," **United States Reports**, Vol. CXLIII, pp. 20-90.

36 Secretary of State, (ed.), **United States Statutes at Large**, Vol. XL, pp. 731.

37 **House Documents, Fifty-ninth Congress, First Session** (Serial 4986) Doc. No. 259, Vol. XLVI, pp. 1-21.

38 **Ibid.**

39 **House Documents, Fifty-eighth Congress, Third Session** (Serial 4829) Doc. No. 38, Vol. L, pp. 1-4.

40 **House Documents, Fifty-ninth Congress, First Session** (Serial 4986) Doc. No. 259, Vol. XLVI, pp. 1-21.

Kidder found that the east end of the Cimarron Base Line, which had been established in 1881 by Channey and Smith, was 1011 feet west of the line which had been surveyed by Clark, and 1754 feet west of the true meridian; he, therefore, concluded that the Clark survey was false by a distance of 734 feet. He was unable to find the monument which designated the intersection of the 100th meridian with the parallel 36 degrees and 30 minutes, but he did locate the Channey and Smith monument which was established 1754 feet west of the meridian and 242 feet south of the parallel of 36 degrees and 30 minutes. Kidder marked the true point of the intersection by a stake without marks, witnessed by a concentric circle pit six feet in diameter and by a mound of carefully sodded earth. He concluded that the resulting differences between his survey and the previous surveys were because of improved methods used in the observation for time and in the exchange of time signals.[41]

Both the United States and Texas had patented lands in the disputed area.[42] In order to adjust the accounts between the public school fund and the public domain fund, the Legislature of Texas designated money which would be received for land which was located in the disputed area to the school fund.[43]

In 1904 the Secretary of Interior drafted a bill which provided that the 100th meridian be re-surveyed.[44] As this bill was rejected by the House, another bill which authorized the President in conjunction with the State of Texas to provide for the marking of the true meridian was recommended by the committee of the judiciary. Congress again demonstrated a lack of interest in the question by its refusal to pass the bill.[45] Conflicting claims between land owners who held title to land from the United States and those who possessed Texas titles continued. In 1911 John L. Wortham, a citizen of Texas made application to the land commissioner of Texas for the survey of a tract of land which was in possession of persons who held patents on the land from the United

41 **Ibid.**

42 **Ibid.**

43 **General Laws of the State of Texas**, Vol. XI, pp. 29-30.

44 **House Executive Documents, Fifty-eighth Congress, Third Session** (serial 4829) Doc. No. 38, Vol. XL, p. 1.

45 **House Reports, Fifty-ninth Congress, First Session** (Serial 4906) Doc. No. 1186, Vol. I, p. 1.

States Government.[46] Official attention was directed to the situation, when on March 1, 1920, Texas, in answering a suit filed by Oklahoma to determine the true boundary along the Red River, held that the line running north from the Kidder initial monument was the true 100th meridian. Oklahoma and the United States claimed that the Jones-Brown-Clark line was the true boundary. The disputed area of approximately 25,000 acres included land patented by the United States to homesteaders; also 2,838 acres were vested in Oklahoma under its school grant while 280 acres were under its university grant.[47] Members of the United States Coast and Geodetric Survey were directed to locate the 100th meridian in 1923 by the most scientific method of triangulation. They located it 371.5 feet east of Kidder's initial point.[48]

In October, 1926, the Supreme Court rule that the Greer County decision did not establish the Jones-Brown-Clark line as the true meridian; the Court said that from 1819 to 1920, there had been no official confirmation of that line.[49] Kidder had never .narked the line from his initial monument which was located at the point where the 100th meridian intersects the Red River. The Court held that twenty-four years was too short a period to give Oklahoma the disputed territory on prescription right; the Supreme Court, consequently, ruled that none of the lines was correct.[50]

On January 3, 1927, the Supreme Court designated Samuel S. Gannett, geodetic and astronomic engineer, to serve as commissioner in supervising the location of the true meridian.[51] On March 5, 1928, the court further stipulated that the line should be run along the true 100th

46 Report of Joint Legislative Committee on Organization and Economy, Texas State Library; Texas Reports, Vol. CXXXIII, pp. 255-260.

47 Minutes of the Oklahoma School Land Commission, School Land Office, Oklahoma City, Oklahoma; "The State of Oklahoma, Complainent versus the State of Texas, Defendant, the United States of America, Intervener," **United States Reports**, Vol. CCLXXII, pp. 713-715.

48 **Ibid.**, p. 21.

49 **Ibid.**, Vol. CLXII, p. 1.

50 **Ibid.**, Vol. CCLXXII, p. 21.

51 **Ibid.**, Vol. CCLXXIII, p. 93.

meridian extending north from its intersection with the south bank of the South Fork of Red River to its intersection with the northern boundary line of the State of Texas as was surveyed by John H. Clark. [52]

In compliance with the request, Gannett started to survey in 1927 and finished it in 1929. By the use of astronomical triangulation, he found that the total length of the boundary line was 133.6 miles. In order to correct any miscalculations, he established check triangulation points every .66 miles. The longest of these offset measurements was 3,620.23 feet and the shortest was 197.78 feet from the meridian. He marked each triangulation stations by a concrete monument and by one or two reference monuments, firmly imbedded in the ground. In the event that any of the boundary monuments on the 100th meridian should be destroyed, it would be an easy matter to re-establish them from the nearest triangulation station. [53]

It was decided that one of the reasons for the discrepancies in the various surveys was caused by the deceptive heat waves mirrored from the deep arroyos and sand hills along its course; in order to avoid this hazard, Gannett made his calculation at night, using the stars as aids along with beacon lights on distant hills. At times, observations were taken on Polaris to check the accuracy of the lines; right angles were turned at the offset points to check the alignment of the farthest visible signal to the south. [54] E.L. McNair, chief of the field party, who did all the instrument work, established 160 monuments over the entire line of 136.6 miles, or a monument every .83rd mile. The monuments were made of concrete molded in galvanized iron forms; 36 inches long, 8 inches in top diameter, 14 inches in base diameter, 12 inches in foundation concrete, usually 24 by 24 by 24 inches. Each monument was reinforced by 3 iron rods 3 feet in length and 3/8 inch in diamenter, set vertically in the base.

Garnett's line was 4,040 feet east of the Jones-Brown-Clark line at the south end and about 880 feet east of that line at the north end. The area of the strip of land included between the lines was approximately 28,500

52 **Ibid.**, Vol. CCLXXVI, p. 596.

53 "The State of Oklahoma, Complainent versus the State of Texas, Defendant, the United States of America Intervener," **Record of the Supreme Court of the United States, October Term, 1929, No. 6 Original,** pp. 1-20.

54 **Ibid.**

acres or 44 and 6/10 square miles.[55] Since this land would certainly be awarded to Texas since Oklahoma had issued titles to much of it, Governor W.J. Holloway of Oklahoma made a desperate effort to purchase this land from Texas before the Supreme Court made final disposition of the case. There was considerable sentiment in Texas in favor of the transfer; a legislative committee negotiated with the Oklahoma Legislature at which time Oklahoma offered 150,000 dollars for 28,000 acres of land. A resolution was introduced in the Texas Senate which provided that the matter be considered, but when the resolution was defeated, all hope of such transfer was abandoned.[56]

On March 14, 1930, the Supreme Court decreed that the boundary line which was delineated and set forth in Gannett's report "Is established and declared to be the true boundary between the states of Texas and Oklahoma along the said meridian."[57]

The State of Texas, therefore, won undisputed title to this strip of 28,500 acres of land. According to the Texas Constitution, public domain may be sold. The Legislature passed a bill which was approved on May 21, 1931, providing for the creation of a commission composed of the Governor, the Attorney General, and the Commissioner of the Land Office, whose duty it was to examine and approve titles which had been issued to owners by the United States Government and by the State of Oklahoma, in order that these title holders might have first choice in securing Texas title. The bill further provided that these claimants would be charged 1.25 dollars per acre for the land.[58]

Before the commission started its work, the heirs of John L. Wortham filed suit against the Texas Land Commissioner for title to the land which he had previously filed on. The Commission postponed action until after the suit was decided in favor of the State of Texas by the Texas

55 **Ibid.**

56 Governor W.J. Holloway to Attorney General R.L. Bobbitt, Oklahoma City, September 23, 1929, "Oklahoma versus Texas," File C, Attorney General's Office, Austin, Texas; R.L. Bobbitt to Governor W.J. Holloway, Austin, Texas, February 13, 1930, Ibid.

57 "the State of Oklahoma, Complainent versus the State of Texas, Defendant, the United States of America Intervener," **United States Reports**, Vol. CCLXXXI, p. III.

58 **Vernon's Civil Statutes of the State of Texas**, Vol. XV, pp. 484-486.

Supreme Court on February 8, 1939.[59] The last meeting of the Commission was held on August 3, 1948; the Commission completed its job by approving an application on the last parcel of land consisting of 76 acres of land in Wheeler County.[60]

The Oklahoma Legislature passed an act in 1941 which provided that the Land Commission allocate claims to lost land to other unallocated tracts in Oklahoma. The purchaser who had lost a part of his land could apply the money which he had paid to the remainder of the land which remained in Oklahoma.[61]

Congressman J.V. McClintic of the Seventh Oklahoma District introduced a bill in the House of Representatives on March 15, 1932, which authorized the Secretary of Interior to ascertain the amount of fees which had been paid by homesteaders to the United States Government for land which had been transferred from the State of Oklahoma to the State of Texas by this decision of March 17, 1930. The bill further provided that these fees be returned with six per cent interest from the time of payment to the passage of the bill.[62] Acting Secretary C. Girard Davidson of the Department of Interior reported on October 21, 1948, that all claimants except three had been reimbursed by an expenditure of 12,488 dollars.[63]

Texas Reports, Vol. CXXXIII, pp. 255-280; Report of the Joint Legislative Committee on Organization and Economy, Texas State Library.

60 Report of the Joint Legislative Committee on Organization and Economy, Texas State Library.

61 **Oklahoma Statutes** (1941), pp. 435-436.

62 **The Daily Oklahoman** (Oklahoma City), March 16, 1932.

63 Acting Secretary C. Girard Davidson of the Department of Interior to C.A. Welborn, of Paris, Texas, Washington, October 21, 1948.

CHAPTER VIII

Controversy Over Channel Of Red River, 1918-1920

Although the territory along Red River including Wichita County, Texas, and Cotton County, Oklahoma, was a highly developed farming region before 1918, the question of boundary was not an important issue. The raising of corn, cotton, and livestock on farms bordering the stream did not necessitate the demarcation of the exact line between the two states. When oil was discovered in the area in 1918, however, interest in the boundary line became a paramount issue; it was found that rich oil deposits were located under the bed of the river. As this immense wealth was at stake, a dispute arose between Texas, Oklahoma, and the United States over the ownership of these deposits.[1]

The State of Texas claimed the south half of the river bed on the assumption that the boundary line followed the center of waterways which marked its boundary. The State therefore issued oil leases to operators who developed producing wells in the bed of the river. Oklahoma claimed title to the entire river bed by reason of the Oklahoma enabling act which established the south boundary of the State along the south bank of Red River;[2] the Oklahoma School Commission consequently sold leases to land claimed by the State of Texas. The Comanche Indians claimed title to the north half of the river bed by virtue of a treaty with the United States Government in which the "Middle of the bed of Red River" was designated as the boundary line;[3] numerous citizens of Texas and Oklahoma claimed that the river bed was Federal

---

1 "Oklahoma versus Texas, United States Intervener," **United States Reports**, Vol. CCLII, p. 372.

2 Secretary of State, (ed.), **Statutes at Large**, Vol. XXXV, Pt. 2, p. 1286.

3 **Ibid.**, Vol. XXXI, p. 677; **ibid.**, Vol. XXXIV, p. 213; **ibid.**, Vol. XXXV, pp. 456-457.

Government land and was therefore subject to placer mining claims.[4]

The claim that the bed of the river was federal property and was therefore subject to placer mining claims was based on the fact that when the Big Pasture Indian Reservation was opened in 1906, the Indians ceded back to the Government, territory from the center of Red River northward.[5] In disposing of this land to settlers, the Government surrendered title from the north bank of the river northward, thereby retaining title to the north one-half of the river bed.[6]

The officials of Texas became concerned over the situation; Attorney General C.M. Cureton in a letter to Governor W.P. Hobby stated that law suits were pending between the state and certain parties who claimed to exercise rights under the authority of the State of Oklahoma and the United States concerning land leases. He recognized the fact that this litigation would be ineffectual in determining the true boundary line. He stated that Oklahoma had authorized the survey and sale of not only the lands in the bed of the river, but thousands of acres of land within the State of Texas, much of which had been patented many years by the State of Texas.

He further informed the Governor that the United States District Attorney in Oklahoma City had brought an action in the United States District Court to restrain the officials of Oklahoma from disposing of the land in the bed of Red River, claiming that the land was property of certain Indian tribes.[7]

In Governor Hobby's message to the Legislature in July, 1919, he recommended that the Legislature adopt a resolution which would authorize the governor and the Attorney General to institute such suits as they might deem necessary in any court for the purpose of establishing and maintaining the rights of the State of Texas, citizens of Texas, and those holding titles from the State of Texas. He further asked for permission to institute suit in the Supreme Court of the United

4 "Oklahoma versus Texas, United States Intervener," **United States Reports**, Vol. CCLII, p. 372; **Dallas Morning News**, March 11, 1919.

5 Secretary of State, (ed.), **Statutes at Large**, Vol. XXXI, p. 677; **ibid.**, Vol. XXXIV, p. 213.

6 **Dallas Morning News**, March 11, 1919.

7 **House Journal, Thirty-sixth Legislature, Second Session**, pp. 597-598.

States for the establishment of the boundary between Oklahoma and Texas.[8]

In response to this request, the Legislature passed a resolution by which the constituted officials of Texas were authorized to institute suit in the Supreme Court of the United States for the purpose of determining the boundary line between the State of Oklahoma and the State of Texas and for the preservation of the rights of its citizens. The Texas officials were further directed to enter suits in any court, state or federal as might be necessary, for the preservation of the rights of its citizens. [9] It was further provided that under the direction of the Governor and Attorney General, the Reclamation Engineer would prepare maps, surveys, profiles, and other data to be used in litigation affecting the Red River boundary.[10]

In 1918-1919 force and intimidation were indiscriminately employed; the courts of both states assumed jurisdiction.[11] At one time in 1919, the militia of Texas was mobilized to enforce an order of a Texas court while a like effort was made to call the Oklahoma militia to enforce a decree of an Oklahoma court.[12]

As a result of the chaos and confusion, the State of Oklahoma filed an original bill against the State of Texas on December 8, 1919, alleging therein that the southern boundary line of Oklahoma, according to the terms of the treaty of February 22, 1819, between the United States and Spain, and as was construed by the Supreme Court in the case of United States versus Texas in 1896,[13] was the south bank of Red River as it existed on February 22, 1819. The attorneys for Oklahoma asked that the court re-affirm this line and that a boundary commission be appoint-

8 **Ibid.**, p. 597.

9 **Ibid.**, p. 598.

10 **Ibid.**, p. 202; **San Antonio Express** (San Antonio, Texas), July 22, 1919.

11 **Daily Oklahoman**, July 27, 1919.

12 "Oklahoma versus Texas, United States Intervener," **United States Reports**, Vol. CCLVIII, p. 280.

13 **Oklahoma Civil Reports**, Vol. XIX, p. 35.

ed to designate the exact line and to delineate upon maps prepared for the purpose, the true boundary as might be determined by the court.[14]

The United States, by permission of the court, intervened. Besides permission to intervene, the United States was authorized to submit a motion to place a receiver in control of the disputed area. Frederick A. Delano was therefore appointed as receiver with power to operate or close wells as he chose, and to collect, conserve, and invest all proceeds after April 1, 1920, as he saw fit. His jurisdiction extended over that part of the bed of the river between the medial line and the south bank with certain east and west limits, covering a distance of 43 miles.[15]

The State of Texas filed an answer on March 1, 1920, in which it denied the finality of that part of the Greer County case of 1896 in which the Supreme Court fixed the boundary line along the south bank of Red River according to the court's interpretation of the treaty of 1819 between the United States and Spain. Texas contended that the signers intended that the line should be along the middle of the stream; that had they not intended that the middle of the river should be the line, they would not have designated the "Course" of the river as the line.[16]

Texas further asserted this claim on the basis of a decision made on April 29, 1897, by an Assistant Attorney General of the United States in which he ruled that the boundary between the Indian Territory and Texas was along the middle of the channel of the river, "As it meandered when Texas was admitted to the Union in 1845."[17] In order to fortify further its contention, the counsel for Texas showed that between 1819 and 1867, the United States negotiated Indian treaties in which the southern boundaries of the lands involved followed the middle of the river; that in no case did the line extend to the south side of the river.[18]

14 "Oklahoma versus Texas, United States Intervener," **United States Reports**, Vol. CCLII, p. 372.

15 **Ibid.**

16 **Ibid.**, Vol. CCLVI, p. 70; **American State Papers, Foreign Relations,** Vol. IV, pp. 623-625.

17 "The State of Oklahoma Complainent versus the State of Texas, Defendant, United States of America Intervener," **Record of the Supreme Court of the United States, October Term, 1920, No. 23 Original,** p. 85.

18 **Ibid., october Term, 1921,** Vol. I, p. 20.

It asserted that should there be no other issue in the case, the fact that Texas had exercised sovereignty and jurisdiction over the south portion of Red River for a long period of years gave the state ownership of the land by the rule of prescription.[19]

By way of counter claim, it was alleged by Texas that the true 100th meridian was not correctly located by Jones, Brown, and Clark but that the true meridian was correctly run by Arthur D. Kidder in 1903, and that the true line was east of the line as it then existed. Texas therefore asked the court to decree the line as located by Kidder as the true line.[20]

On March 20, 1920, the United States filed a petition of intervention by stating that the south bank of Red River was the southern boundary of Oklahoma and that Texas had no right, title, or interest in the land north of that line. Just three months later, the United States and the State of Oklahoma filed a motion requesting the court to set down for hearing upon certain questions of law. On the same day, the Court entered an order designating November 15, 1920, as the date for a hearing to answer the questions as to whether the decree of the Court in the case of the United States versus Texas was final in so far as it declared that the treaty of 1819 established the boundary along the south bank of Red River; and if the decree was not final, to decide whether the treaty established the line along the middle, or along the south bank of the stream.

It further ordered that the parties be permitted to take testimony in respect to the governmental practices on the part of all governments and states concerned in the case. The evidence in chief of the United States and the State of Oklahoma was to be taken on or before August 15, 1920; the evidence in chief of the State of Texas was to be taken on or before October 1, 1920; the rebuttal testimony on the part of the United States and Oklahoma was to be closed on October 20, 1920. The evidence in each case was to be on seven days' notice unless notice should be waived. Ernest Knabel of the District of Columbia was appointed as commissioner to take the evidence and report it to the Court without submitting conclusions.

The defendant reiterated in the answer to the bill of complaint, that because of long and continued possession and usage, the center of the main channel of the Red River had by prescription become a part of the

19 **Supreme Court Reporter**, Sixty-eighty Law Edition, p. 1118.

20 **Ibid.**, p. 1118.

State of Texas,[21] while Oklahoma applied the rule that a line marked and considered by the parties through a long course of years as the boundary line, becomes the true boundary. Oklahoma therefore suggested an examination of the nature and character of the law which would establish the Texas claim to the territory, and then apply the law to the evidence in the case. Counsel for Oklahoma contended that exclusive possession was essential and must be actual, visible, exclusive, notorious, and uninterrupted. It argued that if possession was not actual and exclusive, it lacked two elements that were essential to make an adverse possession; that adverse possession as a basis of title must be exclusive and hostile to all claimants whether they be known or unknown.[22]

To support the claim that possession on the part of Texas was not exclusive and that the United States considered the bed of Red River as United States territory, Oklahoma counsel cited the act of May 26, 1824, which fixed the western boundary of the territory of Arkansas to "begin at a point 40 miles west of the southwest corner of the State of Missouri and run south to the right bank, or south bank of Red River, and thence down that river with the Mexican boundary line to the State of Louisiana."[23]

Oklahoma counsel further offered as evidence in support of its claim that the line followed the south bank; the Spanish Treaty of 1819 which designated the west bank of the Sabine River and the south bank of the Arkansas River, as the boundary line; although the south bank of the Red River was not specifically stated, such was implied by the fact that all the islands throughout the course of the line belonged to the United States.[24] This position was further supported by reference to the Mexican Treaty of 1828;[25] to the terms of the act of December, 1836, by which the Texas Congress recognized this same boundary line;[26] to the

21 **Ibid.**, p. 1118.

22 "Oklahoma versus Texas, United States Intervener," **United States Reports**, Vol. CCLVI, p. 70.

23 Peters, (ed.), **Statutes at Large**, Vol. IV, pp. 40-41.

24 **Ibid.**, Vol. VIII, p. 252.

25 **Ibid.**, p. 372.

26 **Laws of the Republic of Texas**, Vol. I, p. 133.

act of Congress of 1845 which admitted Texas to the Union;[27] to the act by the Congress of May 2, 1890, which described the boundaries of Oklahoma Territory and the boundaries of Indian lands;[28] and by the act which admitted Oklahoma into the Union.[29]

Oklahoma did not deny that Texas had asserted juriscition over the disputed area; it believed that the acts of Oklahoma and the United States were more numerous and were of a more positive character than were the acts of Texas; it contended that these acts of jurisdiction completely nullified the claims of Texas to the area. That Oklahoma had held the south half of the river continuously, openly, and exclusively was substantiated by the fact that the commissioner's court of Montague County considered the south bank of the river as the boundary line;[30] that the Iterior Department of the Federal Government considered the south bank as the line;[31] and that the Land Commissioner of Texas as well as the County Engineers of the boundary counties of Texas terminated their surveys along the south bank line.[32]

The claim of Oklahoma was further supported by the fact that Oklahoma had collected taxes from the Santa Fe; the Kansas, Oklahoma, and Gulf; and the Kansas City, Mexico, and Orient railroads on their bridges from the south bank of the river northward. The Kansas City, Mexico, and Orient had maintained a sign from 1902 to 1923 on the south bank of the river where the road crosses the river from Jackson County, Oklahoma to Hardeman County, Texas, on the south face of which was written "Texas," and on the north face of which was written "Oklahoma." The fact that no effort was made on the part of Texas to remove this sign prior to the filing of the suit was interpreted by Oklahoma counsel as a failure on the part of Texas to prosecute that

27 George Minot, (ed.), **Statutes at Large**, Vol. IX, p. 108.

28 **Ibid.**, Vol. XXVI, p. 81.

29 **Ibid.**, Vol. XXXIV, p. 267.

30 "The State of Oklahoma, Complainent versus the State of Texas, Defendant, United States of America Intervener," **Record of the Supreme Court of the United States, October Term, 1921, No. 28 Original**, p. 199.

31 **Ibid.**, p. 199.

32 **Ibid.**

state's claim.[33]

The Frisco railroad which maintained three bridges across Red River between Texas and Oklahoma, paid taxes on these bridges to Oklahoma; their maps which were prepared for the interstate commerce commission showed the south bank of the river as the boundary line.[34] When the Texas Railroad Commission approved securities upon the properties of the Oklahoma and Gulf railroad, the property was described in the transaction as consisting of 9.1 miles of track from the south bank of Red River to Denison, Texas. The Attorneys for Oklahoma contended that Texas had never collected taxes from any railroad property north of the south bank of the river. They then turned to the question of jurisdiction by pointing out that Oklahoma courts had instructed juries in the trial of criminal cases that the south bank of the river was the boundary line;[35] that Oklahoma laws had been respected by the United States marshall to the south bank;[36] and Texas law southward from that line.[37]

On April 11, 1921, the court ruled that the 1896 construction was conclusive; that in the matter of true location of the boundary, every test that could be applied was "Red Judica," and that the Greer County case determined the entire southern boundary of Oklahoma.[38] As a result of this decision, Texas could advance no claim to the area north of the southern bank, but since the determination as to the location of that bank had not been made, it was possible that some of the oil wells under the receivership would be returned. There were yet four types of claims to be adjusted; Oklahoma grantees and licensees, claims based upon Indian allotments; others who based their claims upon riparian rights to lands which were located on the north bank of the river; and those who

33 **Ibid.**

34 **Ibid.**, p. 521.

35 **Ibid.**, p. 216.

36 **Ibid.**, p. 222.

37 **Ibis.**, p. 264

38 "Oklahoma versus Texas, United States Intervener," **United States Reports**, Vol. CCLVI, p. 70.

held placer mining locations.[39] The United States asserted full title to the south half of the river bed and part interest to the northern half.[40] On June 22, 1922, the Supreme Court declared that the interveners who had asserted claims under the mining laws of the United States had no claim whatever to these lands and that these mining locations had never been valid.[41]

Since Texas had no claim to the bed of the river and since the placer mining claims were not valid, it became necessary to establish the title to the river bed between the two remaining claimants, the United States and the State of Oklahoma. Oklahoma agreed that the Treaty of 1819 gave title to the bed of the river to the United States and that the United States retained such title except that which had been transferred by virtue of the constitution, treaties, or by laws. Oklahoma consequently established claim on the basis of the act by which that state was admitted to the Union, and upon the contention that Red River was a navigable stream.[42]

The attorneys representing Oklahoma undertook to prove that Red River was a navigable stream; they showed that the treaty makers believed that the river was navigable; that they made the treaty with navigability in mind and that they sought to apply to Red River the rule which would govern the boundary line in case of a navigable stream.[43] They presented evidence of heavy traffic on the river after 1819; that many bridges were constructed across the river between 1879 and 1920, all of which were subject to congressional restrictions which applied only

39 These several claims had no relation directly with the boundary line; they related only with proprietary claims to the river bed and with the proceeds from oil and gas in the disputed district.

40 "Oklahoma versus Texas, United States Intervener," **United States Reports**, Vol. CCLVI, p. 70.

41 **Ibid.**, Vol. CCLXXVI, p. 596; **ibid.**, Vol. CCLXXIII, p. 93.

42 A state owns the bed of a navigable stream within its borders while the United States owns beds of non-navigable streams. "Oklahoma versus Texas, United States Intervener," **United States Reports**, Vol. CCLVIII, p. 574.

43 **American State Papers, Foreign Relations**, Vol. IV, pp. 623-625.

to navigable streams. [44] The attorneys for Oklahoma stated that appropriations had been made from time to time for the purpose of cleaning the river for navigation; that by 1915 approximately 350,000 dollars had been spent in the removal of snags, logs, drifts, timber on caving banks, and for dredging and closing chutes behind numerous islands. [45]

The United States admitted that beginning in 1896, Congress had made several appropriations for the purpose of improving that portion of the river between Fulton, Arkansas, and the mouth of the Washita River in Oklahoma; but it pointed out that the officer in charge of the work repeatedly recommended that it was not likely to result in any commercial navigation; that in 1916 the same officer, the Division of Engineers, the Board of Engineers, and the Chief Engineer concurred in the recommendation that the project be abandoned. [46] The reason which they gave for the recommendation was that the high water commerce of earlier periods had disappeared; that the characteristics of the river rendered it impracticalbe to secure a useful channel except by canalization, the cost of which would be prohibitive; that the expenditures already made were practically useless; and that there was no reason to believe that conditions would change in such a way as to bring better results in the future. [47] They pointed out that the same recommendations were repeated in 1921 [48] and that no appropriations had been made for such purpose since 1916, at which time commerce on the river amounted to slightly over 27,000 tons consisting principally of logs and lumber, farm products and general merchandise, most of which moved on the lower reaches of the river. At that time, no steamboats were operating on the upper section of the river and rafting of logs was

44 Secretary of State, (ed.), **Statutes at Large**, Vol. XXV, p. 210; **ibid.**, Vol. XXXIX, Part I, p. 251; **ibid.**, p. 1198; **ibid.**, Vol. XXIV, p. 163; **ibid.**, Vol. XL, p. 339; **ibid.**, Vol. XXXIV, Part I, pp. 8486.

45 "Oklahoma versus Texas, United States Intervener," **United States Reports**, Vol. CCLIII, p. 465.

46 **House Executive Documents, Sixty-fourth Congress, First Session** (Serial 6977) Doc. No. 947, Vol. XXIII, p. 1.

47 **Ibid.**

48 **House Executive Documents, Sixty-seventh Congress, First Session** (Serial 7946) Doc. No. 87, Vol. XIV, p. 1.

negligible.[49]

In spite of the plea of Oklahoma counsel, Justice Willis Van Devanter rendered the decision on May 1, 1922, in which the Court ruled that no part of the river within Oklahoma was navigable; and, therefore, the title of the bed did not pass to the State of Oklahoma upon its admission to the Union. He added that if the State had a claim to any part of this area, it was only such as was incidental to its ownership of riparian lands on the northern bank of the stream.[50] Since Texas had no claim to the river bed and since Oklahoma had no claim to it except as a riparian land owner, the question arose concerning the right of riparian owners on the north side of the river. The right of these riparian owners, if such right existed, extended only to the medial line between the "Cut banks" of the river. Since the boundary line had been designated as the "South Bank,"[51] the principal issue to be determined was whether the line should run along high water mark as the United States and Oklahoma contended, or at low water mark as was insisted upon by Texas.[52]

Many kinds of testimony were offered, much of which was scientific;[53] test by authorities in geology, chemical analysis of the soils, data in regard to the habits of the river in the building of its valleys, as well as testimony of inhabitants and old settlers in regard to the water course and flood stages were taken.[54] Texas showed that the establishment of the boundary line at the foot of the Texas bluffs would include in

49 "Oklahoma versus Texas, United States Intervener," **United States Reports,** Vol. CCLVIII, p. 576.

50 **Ibid.,** p. 575-578.

51 **Ibid.,** Vol. CCLVI, p. 70.

"The State of Oklahoma Complainent versus the State of Texas Defendant, the United States of America Intervener," **Record of the Supreme Court of the United States, October Term, 1921, No. 20, Original,** p. 256.

53 A summary of this evidence is given by E.H. Sellards in "The Oklahoma-Texas Boundary Suit," **Science Magazine,** Vol. VII, p. 347.

54 "The State of Oklahoma Complainent versus the State of Texas, Defendant, the United States of American Intervener," **Record of the Supreme Court of the United States, October Term, 1923, No. 47, Original,** pp. 80-120.

Oklahoma more than 500,000 acres of land located south of the river, including churches, cemeteries, school houses, voting boxes, and farms which had been cultivated for almost 100 years by people whose title to the lands had not been disputed until the discovery of oil on the lands.[55]

On January 15, 1923, the Supreme Court ruled that the treaty of 1819 named three rivers, the Sabine, the Red and the Arkansas in designating the boundary. The Court found that the treaty expressly located the boundary along the western bank of the Sabine River and the southern bank of the Arkansas River; that the intermediate portion as leaving the Sabine at a designated point and running due north until it struck the Red River, then following the course of that river westward to 100 degrees west longitude, then running due north to the Arkansas. The Court said that the words "through the extent of said boundary on their respective banks," were the last by which the treaty provision denoted the relations of the boundary of the rivers, and as those words were otherwise supported, it pointed with controlling force to what was in the minds of the high contracting parties. The court reasoned that it followed from these considerations that the meaning of the treaty provisions were just what it would have been had the Red River section of the boundary been expressly described as along the south bank.

The Court further said that the bed over which the water flowed was composed of light, loose sand and was of varying breadth, the maximum being one and one-half miles and the average one-third of a mile. It found that the valley land was almost uniformly separated from the sand bed of the river by a closely defined water-worn bank, designated by witnesses as a "Cut bank." This bank ranged in height from two to ten feet, the height increasing from west to east and the lower parts usually being where the bed was wide. The "Cut bank" effectively confined the water to the bed, save in exceptional instances when the water was at flood stage and overflowed adjacent lands for short periods at a time. In conclusion, the Court found that the "Cut bank" along the southern side of the sand bed constituted the south bank of the river, and that the boundary was along that bank at the mean level of the water where it washed the bank without overflowing it.[56] This decision, therefore, established ownership of the United States to a narrow strip of land in the bed of Red River between the medial line of that stream and the southern "Cut bank." The claims of all litigants had thus far been

55 **Ibid.**, pp. 51-53.

56 "Oklahoma versus Texas, United States Intervener," **United States Reports**, Vol. CCLXI, pp. 340-352.

established except those who based their claims upon Indian allotments.

According to the terms of the Kiowa-Comanche-Apache Treaty of 1867,[57] the Indians were given title to lands bounded on the south by the middle of the north Fork and on the east by 98 degrees west longitude. These lands were held in common until June 6, 1900, when 160 acres were allotted to each member of the tribes; 2,480,000 acres of grazing land was set aside as a reserve for the common use of the tribes, and four sections in each township were designated for school and other purposes; the remaining land came under the public land laws. Like the treaty, the land act described the southern limits as the middle of the river channel.[58]

The reserve was subsequently disposed of by an act of June 5, 1906, which provided that each child born in the tribes after 1900 was to be given 160 acres. The remainder of the land was made subject to entry and sale. Thus all the region on the north side of Red River between 98 degrees west longitude and the North Fork of Red River was disposed of by 1906. Some of the lands were allotted to Indians, some became Oklahoma school land, while still another portion was opened to white settlers.[59]

All riparian claims on the north side of the river were founded upon these disposals. The patents to the various disposals did not express either the inclusion or exclusion of the rights of the posessors to the river bed. The question as to whether the state line shifted with the channel; and what was the status of the riparian rights to the owner whose land became a part of the river bed; and did the non-riparian owner before the change thereafter become a riparian owner, became paramount issues in the question.

A partial decree in regard to these questions was entered on March 12, 1923, which stipulated that the boundary was the same as that which existed in 1921; that where evulsion had occurred, the boundary was identical with that of 1921, and where the river had cut a secondary channel through adjacent plains on the south side of the river in such a way that land theretofore had become an island, the boundary would be along the north bank of the islands so created. The Court further ruled that where by accretion or erosion, there had been subsequent changes in the bank, the boundary line changed with the channel of the river.

The Court clarified the definition of the south bank by stating that the

58 **Ibid.**

59 "Oklahoma versus Texas, United States Intervener," **United States Reports**, Vol. CCLVIII, p. 574.

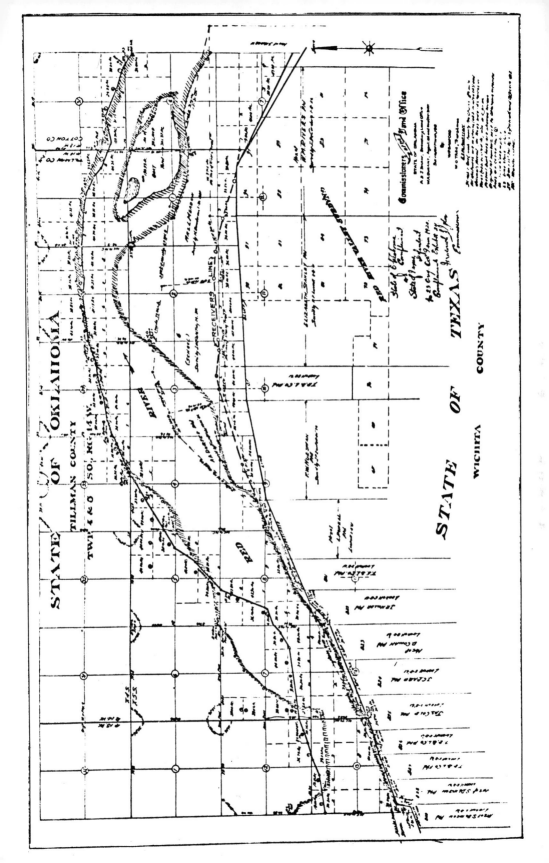

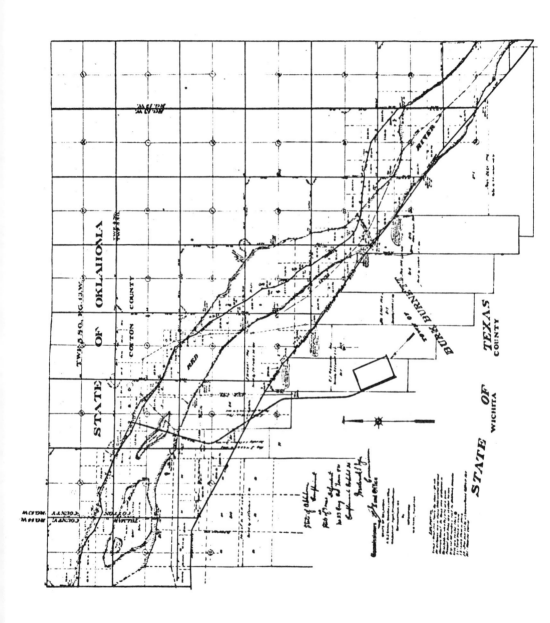

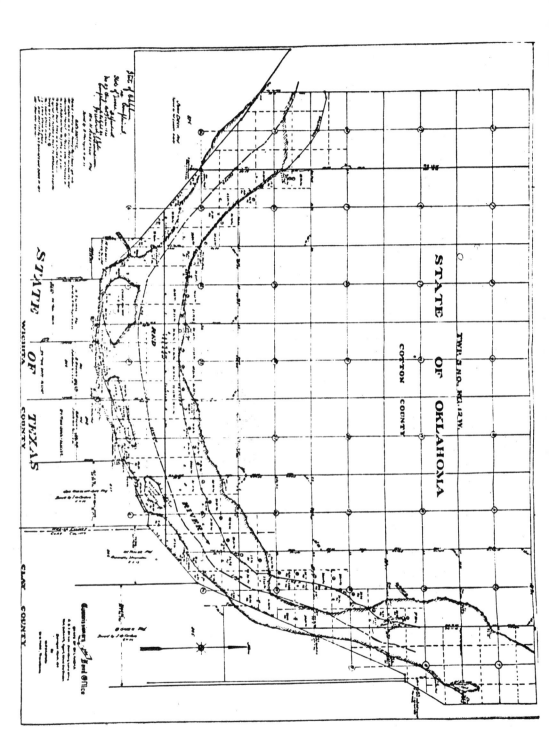

main level of the waters on the south bank was the boundary; that where the south bank inclined, the boundary was the line over such incline which conformed to the mean level of the waters when at places in that vicinity, they washed the cut bank without overflowing it. The court also acted to remove a serious problem on the part of Texas by guaranteeing to that State a reasonable access to the river.

The court authorized Arthur D. Kidder and A.A. Stiles to mark the line along the Big Bend area,[60] westward to the south extension of the west line of range 16 in Oklahoma. The line in every instance was to be located and marked along the south bank as it existed in 1921. It was further ordered that the region about Big Bend be surveyed first and that all oil wells within 300 feet of both sides of the line be noted. The cost of the survey was to be divided between Texas and Oklahoma, and between Texas and the United States; the line which was to be established was subject to the approval of the Court. It was further ordered that copies of the report be sent to the two states and that all exceptions or objections be placed before the Clerk of the Court within 40 days.[61]

A supplement to the partial decree of June 5, 1922, was also entered on March 12, 1923, which provided that interveners were allowed possession to the middle of the river unless otherwise directed; that tracts which were non-riparian when they were surveyed and had become riparian since, were extended to the middle of the river unless lands in front of them had been previously disposed of. Tracts which had become a part of the river bed after the survey and before disposal, which were patented or allotted as upland while nearby lands behind them were then unsold and unallotted, carried title to the middle of the river provided that other tracts between them and the line had not been disposed of previously. The receiver, according to this decree was ordered to surrender as quickly as possible all patented and allotted tracts on the north side of the mid-channel which were within the receivership area and were void of oil wells.[62] An order entered on June 4, 1923, directed the boundary commission, in addition to other assignments, to survey and plot the mid-channel of the river in the

60 The bend in the river which separates Clay County, Texas, and Cotton County, Oklahoma, was referred to as "Big Bend."

61 "Oklahoma versus Texas, United States Intervener," **United States Reports**, Vol. CCLXI, pp. 345-351.

62 **Ibid.**, Vol. CCLXI, p. 345.

region of the oil wells which included an area three miles in length; the expenses of the survey were to be charged to the receivership.[63] The reports of this commission were ordered filed on April 25, 1924; all exceptions were to be made before May 23, 1924.[64]

On June 9, 1924, the Court decreed that general expenses of the receivership were apportionable against the several funds derived by the receiver from operation of gas and oil wells on both sides of the boundary; that funds accruing from wells operated by claimants under the receivers' supervision should be assessed on a lower basis than funds arising from wells operated by him directly. It was further provided that the receiver should make charges against each fund as a whole. The expense of unproductive wells located in the river bed area which belonged to the United States was to be charged to the receivership. Those who had trespassed before the institution of the receivership would have no claim to be compensated for the cost of these wells out of the profits form productive wells.[65]

The receiver was then ordered to have his accounts audited by June 30, 1924, and to pay a Texas production tax.[66] On November 18, 1924, the Court decreed that the receiver was not subject to the tax upon producing wells. The receiver, however, was directed to pay taxes on proceeds belonging to those persons who were out of state or were insolvent during the period of the receivership. In conclusion, the Court directed the receiver to prepare to terminate the receivership.[67] The report of the receiver was approved on June 1, 1925, at which time the receivership was declared at an end. Just three days later, the Court confirmed the report of the boundary commission on the surveys that had been made from 100 degrees west longitude to the eastern limits of Lamar County, Texas.[68] This survey was subsequently continued to the eastern limit of Oklahoma; the final report was approved and the commission was discharged on April 25, 1927.[69]

63 **Ibid.**, Vol. CCLXII, p. 505.

65 **Ibid.**, Vol. CCLXVII, pp. 602-609.

66 **Ibid.**, Vol. CCLXII, p. 724.

67 **Ibid.**, Vol. CCLXVII, p. 580.

68 **Ibid.**, Vol. CCLXIX, p. 314.

69 **Ibid.**, Vol. CCLXXIV, pp. 713-714.

This dispute was an example of a state's reliance upon the customary opinion that the middle of a stream is the boundary between two political units instead of adhering to a definite provision of a treaty when valuable mineral deposits are at stake. Although the treaty of 1819 did not specifically state that the United States would possess the islands without the possession of the river bed. The individuals who obtained title to the land by spurious means demonstrated the attitude that if the government possesses land, the individual may secure it by the asking. In spite of the efforts of the negotiators of the treaty of 1819 to establish a boundary line which would be so clear, so specific, and so recognizable that no dispute could ever arise, that portion of the boundary along the 100 meridian and along Red River became one of the most noted boundary disputes in the history of the United States.